# Survey of Credit Underwriting Practices 2009

## Office of the Comptroller of Currency
## July 2009

# Contents

Introduction ................................................................................................................... 1

**Part I: Overall Results** ............................................................................................ 2
    Primary Findings ....................................................................................................... 2
    Commentary on Credit Risk ...................................................................................... 3
    Commercial Underwriting Standards ....................................................................... 4
    Retail Underwriting Standards .................................................................................. 9

**Part II: Data Graphs** ............................................................................................... 12
    Overall Annual Change in Loan Production ........................................................... 13
    Sources of Loan Production Change ........................................................................ 14
    Overall Commercial Credit Underwriting Trends ................................................... 15
    Commercial Underwriting Trends, by Product Type ............................................... 16
    Commercial Underwriting Trends, by Product Type (cont'd) ................................. 17
    Reasons for Tightening Commercial Underwriting Standards ................................. 18
    Methods Used to Tighten Commercial Underwriting Standards .............................. 19
    Commercial Credit Risk Trends (Past 12 Months and Next 12 Months) ................. 20
    Commercial Credit Risk Trends (Current Credit Risk Change, by Product Type) ....... 21
    Commercial Credit Risk Trends (cont'd) ................................................................ 22
    Overall Retail Credit Underwriting Trends ............................................................ 23
    Retail Underwriting Trends, by Product Type ........................................................ 24
    Reasons for Tightening Retail Underwriting Standards .......................................... 25
    Methods Used to Tighten Retail Underwriting Standards ....................................... 26
    Retail Credit Risk Trends (Past 12 Months and Next 12 Months) .......................... 27
    Retail Credit Risk Trends (Current Credit Risk Change, by Product Type) ............ 28
    Origination Purpose ................................................................................................. 29
    Residential Real Estate Lending Origination Channels ........................................... 30

**Part III: Data Tables** .............................................................................................. 31
    Commercial Lending Portfolios ............................................................................... 32
        Agricultural Lending ........................................................................................ 32
        Asset-Based Loans ........................................................................................... 33
        Commercial Leasing ........................................................................................ 34
        Commercial Real Estate Lending—Commercial Construction ....................... 35
        Commercial Real Estate Lending—Residential Construction ........................ 36
        Commercial Real Estate Lending—Other ....................................................... 37
        International Lending ........................................................................................ 38
        Middle Market Lending .................................................................................... 39
        Small Business Lending .................................................................................... 40
        Leveraged Loans .............................................................................................. 41
        Large Corporate Loans ..................................................................................... 42
        Hedge Funds (Direct Credit Exposure) ........................................................... 43
        Hedge Funds (Counterparty Credit Exposure) ............................................... 44

Retail Lending Portfolios ........................................................................................... 45
  Affordable Housing Lending ................................................................................. 45
  Credit Card Lending ............................................................................................. 46
  Other Direct Consumer Lending ........................................................................... 47
  Home Equity—Conventional Lending ................................................................. 48
  Home Equity—High LTV Lending ....................................................................... 49
  Indirect Consumer Lending .................................................................................. 50
  Residential Real Estate Lending ........................................................................... 51

# Survey of Credit Underwriting Practices
# 2009

## Introduction

The Office of the Comptroller of the Currency (OCC) conducted its 15th annual underwriting survey to identify trends in lending standards and credit risk for the most common types of commercial and retail credit offered by national banks. The survey covers the 12-month period ending March 31, 2009.

The 2009 survey includes examiner assessments of credit underwriting standards at the 59 largest national banks with assets of $3 billion or more. This population covers loans totaling $3.6 trillion as of December 2008, approximately 84 percent of total loans in the national banking system. Large banks referenced in the subsequent comments are the 15 largest banks by asset size supervised by the OCC's Large Bank Supervision department; the other 44 banks are supervised by the OCC's Midsize/Community Bank Supervision department.

OCC examiners assigned to each bank assessed overall credit trends for 20 commercial and retail credit products. For purposes of this survey, commercial credit includes the following 13 categories:
- agricultural.
- asset-based lending.
- commercial construction.
- residential construction.
- other commercial real estate.
- commercial leasing.
- international.
- large corporate.
- leveraged.
- middle market.
- small business.
- hedge funds – direct lending exposure.
- hedge funds – counterparty credit exposure.

Retail credit includes the following seven categories:
- affordable housing.
- credit cards.
- indirect consumer paper.
- conventional home equity.
- high loan-to-value (HLTV) home equity.
- other direct consumer.
- residential first mortgages.

The term "underwriting standards," as used in this report, refers to the terms and conditions under which banks extend or renew credit, such as financial and collateral requirements, repayment programs, maturities, pricing, and covenants. Conclusions about "easing" or "tightening" represent OCC examiners' observations during the survey period. A conclusion that the underwriting standards for a particular loan category have eased or tightened does not necessarily indicate that all the standards for that particular category have been adjusted. Rather, it suggests that the adjustments that did occur had the net effect of easing or tightening the aggregate conditions under which banks extended credit.

Part I of this report summarizes the overall findings of the survey. Part II depicts the survey findings in data graphs. Part III presents the raw data used to develop the survey findings and to create the data graphs.

# Part I: Overall Results

## *Primary Findings*

- Findings that were reported in the 2008 survey continued through March 2009, as the majority of the banks surveyed tightened underwriting standards for both commercial and retail loans. This tightening offsets widespread easing that was reported in the surveys for 2004 through 2007 and is a measured response to a slowing economy and pockets of deteriorating product performance.
- Despite tightening of underwriting standards as noted in the 2009 survey, banks continue to extend credit in commercial and retail loan products. Examiners reported that 37 percent of the banks in the survey increased loan production since the 2008 survey, while 31 percent experienced no measurable change in loan volume.
- Loan portfolios that experienced the most tightening in underwriting during the 2009 survey period include home equity, residential and commercial construction, followed by international lending and lending to hedge funds.
- As expected, the economy was a major factor in the 2009 survey findings. Examiners reported that the economy was the most important credit issue confronting banks, in addition to being the primary reason changes were made to underwriting standards.
- Examiners identified the following additional factors that affected loan production and underwriting standards: Depressed real estate market, changes in risk appetite, refinancing concerns, and the impact that relaxed underwriting standards from prior years had on payment performance.
- The level of credit risk in both commercial and retail portfolios was reported to have increased since the previous survey year and is projected to increase over the next 12 months.
- This year's survey indicates that the majority of banks now use generally the same underwriting standards regardless of the intent to hold or distribute. A key lesson learned from the financial market disruption is the need for bankers to apply sound, consistent underwriting standards regardless of whether a loan is originated with the intent to hold or sell. The OCC reminds bankers that underwriting standards should not be compromised by competitive pressures or the assumption that the loan will be sold to third parties.

## Commentary on Credit Risk

The financial market disruption continues to affect bankers' appetite for risk and has resulted in a renewed focus on fundamental credit principles by bank lenders. For the 12 months covered by the 2009 survey, examiners reported tightening of underwriting standards in 86 percent of the surveyed banks compared with 52 percent in the 2008 survey. The tightening of standards reported in the last two surveys reflects concerns about unfavorable external conditions and product performance. On a product-by-product basis, tightening was most significant for commercial real estate, large corporate, middle market, small business, residential real estate, home equity, and indirect products.

Once again, examiners reported that the surveyed banks used pricing as their primary method to modify underwriting standards for commercial products. However, loan covenants and collateral requirements were also used to tighten standards. Covenants, as well as other structural underwriting criteria, afford banks a greater measure of control in managing credit risk.

For retail products, collateral requirements, advance rates, and score card cutoffs were the principal methods used to tighten underwriting standards.

As was the case in the 2008 survey, examiners cited the current economic outlook as the primary reason for tightening standards for both commercial and retail products. Changes in risk appetite, product performance, or portfolio quality are additional reasons for tightening standards.

Similar to changing underwriting standards, the decision to introduce or discontinue a product or line of business indicates change in a bank's risk appetite. During the 2009 survey period, most of the new or discontinued product activity occurred in the retail arena. Twelve banks (20 percent) discontinued or plan to discontinue one or more retail related mortgage products. Ten banks (17 percent) have or will exit indirect marine and recreational vehicle (RV) lending and four banks (7 percent) have or will exit other direct consumer lending.

The actions taken to tighten standards in the past two years have done little to offset the cumulative effect of easing and the migration toward high-yielding and higher risk products that occurred in several previous years. These factors, as well as uncertainty about the economy, contributed to examiners' assessments about the level of current and prospective risk in retail and commercial portfolios.

The overall level of credit risk, as reported by examiners, increased in both retail and commercial portfolios. Further, they expect risk to continue increasing over the coming 12 months. Examiners indicated concerns with *current* levels of risk in all real estate products, large corporate loans, leveraged finance, other direct consumer, and small business products. However, the level of credit risk was deemed to be increasing in all loan products offered. This increased risk is due primarily to continued concerns with the economy, escalating job losses, and decreased real estate values.

## Commercial Underwriting Standards

After years of eased underwriting standards, examiners reported a continuation of the 2008 survey's findings of tightening commercial credit standards for the 12 months ending March 31, 2009. The 2009 survey results indicate that more than 86 percent of the surveyed banks tightened commercial underwriting standards, while none reported any easing of standards.

| Commercial Products | | | | | |
|---|---|---|---|---|---|
| | **2005** | **2006** | **2007** | **2008** | **2009** |
| Eased | 34% | 31% | 26% | 6% | 0% |
| Unchanged | 54% | 63% | 58% | 42% | 14% |
| Tightened | 12% | 6% | 16% | 52% | 86% |

Examiners cited the economic outlook and risk appetite as the primary reasons for tightened standards across all product lines. Secondary reasons came from changes in risk appetite and concerns with loan performance or portfolio quality. While the economic outlook was a main concern for all commercial products, it continues to be the most pronounced for commercial real estate (CRE) products. For larger institutions, the disruption in financial markets that began in the second half of 2007 had a significant impact on the leveraged finance and syndicated loan markets; the disruption continued through the end of the 2009 survey period. The lack of liquidity in secondary markets is considered a material contributing factor for tightened standards for large corporate, middle market and leveraged loans.

Credit spreads, or the compensation for assuming credit risk, continues to be the primary underwriting method that banks use to manage the credit risk in their loan portfolios. However, banks have also increased the use of covenants, collateral, guarantor support, and size of credit lines to control risks in their portfolios.

### Selected Product Trends

Underwriting standards tightened for all commercial loan products surveyed. The most prevalent tightening occurred in CRE loans, middle market, small business, and large corporate loans. Examiners reported a few isolated instances of eased commercial credit underwriting standards in asset-based and other CRE products.

#### Commercial Real Estate

CRE products include commercial residential construction, commercial construction, and other CRE loans. These products are offered by virtually all of the surveyed banks. CRE remains a primary concern among examiners, given the rapid growth of these exposures and banks' significant concentrations relative to their capital. Net tightening, which measures the difference between the percentage of banks tightening compared with those easing, was greatest in commercial residential construction, followed by commercial construction and other commercial real estate.

Examiners most often cited the following reasons for strengthening of CRE underwriting standards:

- Continued weakening in the economy; more specifically, the downturn in real estate markets.
- Declines in market values and prices as a result of oversupply or slow-moving inventory.
- Change in risk appetite based on internal and external factors.
- Performance and quality of loans in the portfolio and accompanying risk associated with those loans.

Examiners indicated that overall CRE credit risk increased at 96 percent of the banks since the previous survey and is expected to increase during the next survey year at 98 percent of the banks. Driving the assessment of increased credit risk are external conditions, downward trends in collateral values, weakening debt service capacity, and current and expected levels of problem loans.

The next three tables provide the breakdown by each real estate type.

Thirty-nine banks (or 66 percent) of the 59 banks in the survey offer commercial residential construction loan products. Examiners noted that the slow moving home sales and depressed home values are delaying the recovery in the housing market. Certain markets, notably Florida, California, Arizona, and Nevada, have seen a more pronounced deterioration than the rest of the country. Foreclosures continue to escalate, and banks are reducing their exposure in residences with one to four units and condos in light of the weak economic environment and high levels of nonperforming, criticized/classified assets, and losses. The following table shows that 92 percent of banks surveyed for the 2009 survey tightened underwriting standards for commercial residential construction while none reported easing standards.

| Commercial Residential Construction | | | | | |
|---|---|---|---|---|---|
| | **2005** | **2006** | **2007** | **2008** | **2009** |
| Eased | 21% | 25% | 17% | 2% | 0% |
| Unchanged | 72% | 64% | 50% | 36% | 8% |
| Tightened | 7% | 11% | 33% | 62% | 92% |

Examiners reported that the continued economic downturn, job losses, and a decline in consumer spending are adversely affecting retail, office, and industrial sectors and are receiving elevated attention by 46 of the banks in the survey. Retail properties had the most concerns raised by examiners because of declining consumer confidence and spending levels, weak retail sales, increased store closings, and increased numbers of bankruptcy and liquidations in the retail sector.

Examiners indicated that the multifamily sector seems to be holding its own; however, some major metropolitan areas may see apartment rentals adversely affected by job losses. In addition, the lack of a commercial mortgage-backed securities (CMBS) market has reduced availability of term financing by the securitization market reflecting concern over significant drops in property cash flows and a higher incidence of tenant defaults. The following table shows that 80 percent of banks surveyed this report tightened underwriting standards for commercial construction while none reported easing standards.

| Commercial Construction | | | | | |
|---|---|---|---|---|---|
| | **2005** | **2006** | **2007** | **2008** | **2009** |
| Eased | 29% | 32% | 29% | 8% | 0% |
| Unchanged | 63% | 56% | 59% | 43% | 20% |
| Tightened | 8% | 12% | 13% | 49% | 80% |

As with commercial residential and commercial construction, examiners reported that this sector's declining values, increasing vacancy and significant reduction in permanent market liquidity has triggered a change in risk appetite. In some cases, failed syndications have resulted in banks retaining a higher level of originated loans on their balance sheets. The following table shows that 76 percent of banks surveyed tightened underwriting standards for other CRE while 2 percent reported easing standards.

| Other CRE | | | | | |
|---|---|---|---|---|---|
| | **2005** | **2006** | **2007** | **2008** | **2009** |
| Eased | 24% | 32% | 20% | 2% | 2% |
| Unchanged | 65% | 60% | 73% | 73% | 22% |
| Tightened | 11% | 8% | 7% | 25% | 76% |

Middle Market Loans

Examiners reported a significant change in underwriting standards at 42 of the 59 banks that had middle market loan portfolios since last year's survey. The move to more conservative underwriting by the banks is driven by increasing credit problems, the impact of the recession on businesses, less competition, and decreased liquidity in the market. Examiners reported that banks are attempting to control credit risk and limit potential losses in this portfolio. Comments made indicate that banks are concerned that as the economy worsens, middle market companies will have deteriorating financial performance, which will affect cash flow and overall staying power of these companies.

The level of credit risk in middle market loans increased at 92 percent of the banks with this product. Examiners expect this risk to increase over the next 12 months at 96 percent of the banks. As with other sectors, the economy is the driving factor in examiners' increased risk assessment. However, concerns were also noted with the employment outlook, increases in classified loans and past due trends. The following table shows that 67 percent of banks surveyed tightened underwriting standards for middle market loans while none reported easing standards.

| Middle Market Loans | | | | | |
|---|---|---|---|---|---|
| | **2005** | **2006** | **2007** | **2008** | **2009** |
| Eased | 28% | 31% | 33% | 6% | 0% |
| Unchanged | 67% | 66% | 60% | 69% | 33% |
| Tightened | 6% | 3% | 7% | 25% | 67% |

## Small Business Loans

Examiners reported that 42 of the 59 surveyed banks tightened standards in their small business products. We note that there are varying definitions of small business lending among the surveyed banks. However, regardless of definitional variances, examiners reported tightened underwriting standards and increased risk for small business in line with other surveyed products. Examiners cited changes in the company's financial condition, combined with the economic outlook, as the major reasons for tightened credit.

Examiners indicated that small business credit risk increased at 84 percent of the banks since the prior survey, and expect the risk will continue to increase over the next year at 95 percent of the banks. Changes in external conditions and portfolio quality were the reasons most frequently cited to support the assessment for this increased level of risk. The following table shows that 64 percent of banks surveyed tightened underwriting standards for small business loans while none reported easing standards.

| Small Business Loans | | | | | |
|---|---|---|---|---|---|
| | **2005** | **2006** | **2007** | **2008** | **2009** |
| Eased | 13% | 19% | 11% | 11% | 0% |
| Unchanged | 81% | 76% | 77% | 72% | 36% |
| Tightened | 6% | 5% | 13% | 17% | 64% |

## Large Corporate Loans

Before the market disruption of late 2007, institutional investors heavily influenced underwriting standards in this market segment. However, because of weaknesses in the economy, the lack of secondary market liquidity, less competition, and declining portfolio quality, examiners reported that banks tightened standards and are being more conservative in their lending practices. Other factors contributing to tighter standards include the possible trickle down impact of the real estate problems on this sector, coupled with increased economic risk in companies associated with automotive and retail. Examiners at 35 of the 59 banks in the survey reported that banks are looking for borrowers with stronger balance sheets with diversified cash flows, with a goal of reducing risk in this portfolio.

Examiners reported that credit risk in this product increased at 86 percent of the banks since last year's survey and expect this risk to increase at 97 percent of the banks over the next year. The economic recession and the corresponding impact on borrowers remains as the principal driver on risk within the portfolio. Examiners stated that credit risk will likely increase as many borrowers attempt to downsize their operations to adjust to economic challenges within their industry sector. Because of the challenges facing these borrowers, examiners expect that the levels of criticized and classified credits in these portfolios are likely to increase through 2009. The following table shows that 60 percent of banks surveyed tightened underwriting standards for large corporate loans while none reported easing standards.

| Large Corporate Loans | | | | | |
|---|---|---|---|---|---|
| | **2005** | **2006** | **2007** | **2008** | **2009** |
| Eased | 32% | 49% | 40% | 6% | 0% |
| Unchanged | 68% | 51% | 60% | 62% | 40% |
| Tightened | 0% | 0% | 0% | 32% | 60% |

## Originate to Hold Versus Originate to Sell

This is the second annual survey to assess the differences in underwriting between loans originated to hold in the banks' own loan portfolios and loans originated to sell in the marketplace. Of the 59 banks surveyed, 29 percent originated loans both to hold or to sell. In this year's survey, examiners indicate that the majority (86 percent) of the banks originated loans in the various product lines with generally the same underwriting standards regardless of intent to hold or distribute. When standards differed, banks typically mitigated risks of loss through conservative limits on exposures held. These limits were breached in some banks when secondary market liquidity declined.

The most notable difference in underwriting standards in this year's survey is for leveraged loans. While most leveraged loans underwritten with the intent to sell were underwritten on the same terms as those held for investment, examiners observed a higher incidence of leveraged loans underwritten differently than was observed for other loans types. New leveraged loan volume was low in the 2009 survey. Examiners noted that loans underwritten in the current market were generally more conservatively underwritten as evidenced by reduced leverage, higher debt service coverage, and increased loan covenants. The continued tightening of underwriting standards for all loans, whether intended for sale or investment, is a direct result of changes in the economic outlook and market liquidity.

| 2008 Survey Results | | |
|---|---|---|
| **Product** | **Underwritten Differently** | |
| | **Yes** | **No** |
| Leveraged Loans | 67% | 33% |
| Agricultural | 50% | 50% |
| International | 40% | 60% |
| Asset-Based Loans | 33% | 67% |
| Large Corporate | 21% | 79% |
| CRE – Commercial Residential Construction | 17% | 83% |
| CRE – Commercial Construction | 20% | 80% |
| CRE – Other | 20% | 80% |

| 2009 Survey Results | | |
|---|---|---|
| **Product** | **Underwritten Differently** | |
| | **Yes** | **No** |
| Leveraged Loans | 38% | 62% |
| Asset-Based Loans | 13% | 87% |
| Large Corporate | 21% | 79% |
| CRE – Commercial Residential Construction | 17% | 83% |
| CRE – Commercial Construction | 10% | 90% |
| CRE – Other | 9% | 91% |

## *Retail Underwriting Standards*

Examiners reported continued tightening in retail underwriting standards in the 2009 survey, citing economic factors as the major basis for the change. Tightened standards were noted in 83 percent of the reporting banks, up from 68 percent in last year's survey. None reported easing retail underwriting standards.

| Retail Products | | | | |
|---|---|---|---|---|
| | **2006** | **2007** | **2008** | **2009** |
| Eased | 28% | 20% | 0% | 0% |
| Unchanged | 65% | 67% | 32% | 17% |
| Tightened | 7% | 13% | 68% | 83% |

In cases when underwriting standards were tightened, examiners noted that banks frequently cited more stringent collateral requirements, closely followed by scorecard changes, pricing and loan fees, and debt service requirements. This conclusion is based primarily on responses relative to real estate lending products, the most prevalent products offered by the surveyed banks. Survey results also indicated a reduction in the types of mortgage products offered. No surveyed banks offered payment option adjustable rate mortgages during the survey year.

Examiners indicated that there was lower tolerance for underwriting exceptions for all types of retail credit. Easing was noted for only one product in one bank, representing less than one percent of total responses.

Examiners reported increased retail credit risk in at least one product at 56 of the 58 banks that offered retail products. This increased level of risk was most pronounced in home equity, indirect consumer, and credit card lending. Examiners cited concerns about general economic conditions and portfolio performance resulting from prior years' liberal underwriting as the basis for increased risk levels. Examiners expect retail credit risk to continue to increase over the next 12 months at 87 percent of the banks, particularly in home equity and credit card portfolios.

## Selected Product Trends

In this year's survey, examiners reported continued tightening of credit standards in a significant number of the surveyed retail loan products. In fact, the responses indicated tightened standards for 71 percent of retail loan products, and no change in the standards for 29 percent. Examiners noted easing of standards for less than 1 percent of retail loan products.

### Residential Real Estate

As shown in the next three tables, tighter underwriting standards were prevalent in residential real estate and home equity lending products. No banks eased standards in any of these products. Examiners stated that underwriting standards tightened mainly because of the dramatic changes in economic conditions and poor portfolio performance brought on by more liberal underwriting standards in prior years, particularly 2005 through 2007 originations.

Some banks responded to the current residential real estate downturn by ceasing to offer certain products. For example, all 14 of the banks that had previously offered high LTV home equity loans either exited the product in the last 12 months or are planning to do so in the next 12 months. Fewer banks—six of the 52 banks with the product—have exited or will exit residential real estate mortgage lending. Similarly, three of 51 reporting banks have exited or will exit conventional home equity lending. As shown below, ninety-three percent of banks surveyed tightened underwriting standards for high LTV home equity loans; 73 percent for residential real estate, and 78 percent for conventional home equity lending. None reported easing standards.

| Home Equity – High LTV | | | | |
|---|---|---|---|---|
| | 2006 | 2007 | 2008 | 2009 |
| Eased | 37% | 22% | 6% | 0% |
| Unchanged | 63% | 61% | 6% | 7% |
| Tightened | 0% | 17% | 89% | 93% |

| Residential Real Estate | | | | |
|---|---|---|---|---|
| | 2006 | 2007 | 2008 | 2009 |
| Eased | 26% | 19% | 0% | 0% |
| Unchanged | 69% | 67% | 44% | 27% |
| Tightened | 5% | 14% | 56% | 73% |

| Home Equity – Conventional | | | | |
|---|---|---|---|---|
| | 2006 | 2007 | 2008 | 2009 |
| Eased | 34% | 19% | 2% | 0% |
| Unchanged | 64% | 66% | 46% | 22% |
| Tightened | 2% | 16% | 52% | 78% |

<u>Indirect Consumer Lending</u>

Tighter underwriting standards were prevalent in indirect consumer lending products. Much like real estate related lending, examiners stated that underwriting standards tightened mainly because of the dramatic changes in economic conditions and poor portfolio performance brought on by more liberal underwriting standards in prior years, particularly 2005 through 2007.

Twenty-seven of the surveyed banks offer indirect consumer lending products. Of those, 14 banks (or 52 percent) either exited the product in the last 12 months, or will within the next 12 months. The following table shows that 74 percent of banks surveyed tightened underwriting standards for indirect consumer lending. No banks eased standards in this product.

| Indirect Consumer Lending | | | | |
|---|---|---|---|---|
| | **2006** | **2007** | **2008** | **2009** |
| Eased | 35% | 16% | 20% | 0% |
| Unchanged | 52% | 75% | 56% | 26% |
| Tightened | 13% | 9% | 24% | 74% |

## **Originate to Hold Versus Originate to Sell**

National banks originate most retail credit products to hold. At the product level, 69 percent of products were originated exclusively to hold. Another 28 percent of the products were originated both to hold and to sell. Only 3 percent were originated exclusively to sell. These percentages are unchanged from the 2008 survey. Products held and sold, and sold only, consist primarily of residential mortgage and affordable housing loans. Surveyed banks typically originated residential mortgage and home equity loans in their retail branches. Broker and correspondent channels combined accounted for 14 percent of residential mortgage originations and 5 percent of home equity loans.

In most banks that originated both to hold and to sell, the underwriting standards for the two groups of originations did not differ. In banks whose underwriting standards for the two groups did differ, the primary differences were in pricing and fees.

# Part II: Data Graphs

Overall Annual Change in Loan Production ........................................................................13
Sources of Loan Production Change ...............................................................................14
Overall Commercial Credit Underwriting Trends..............................................................15
Commercial Underwriting Trends, by Product Type........................................................16
Commercial Underwriting Trends, by Product Type (cont'd) ..........................................17
Reasons for Tightening Commercial Underwriting Standards .........................................18
Methods Used to Tighten Commercial Underwriting Standards ......................................19
Commercial Credit Risk Trends (Past 12 Months and Next 12 Months) ........................20
Commercial Credit Risk Trends (Current Credit Risk Change, by Product Type)............21
Commercial Credit Risk Trends (cont'd)..........................................................................22
Overall Retail Credit Underwriting Trends........................................................................23
Retail Underwriting Trends, by Product Type ..................................................................24
Reasons for Tightening Retail Underwriting Standards....................................................25
Methods Used to Tighten Retail Underwriting Standards .................................................26
Retail Credit Risk Trends (Past 12 Months and Next 12 Months)....................................27
Retail Credit Risk Trends (Current Credit Risk Change, by Product Type) ......................28
Origination Purpose..........................................................................................................29
Residential Real Estate Lending Origination Channels ...................................................30

# Overall Annual Change in Loan Production

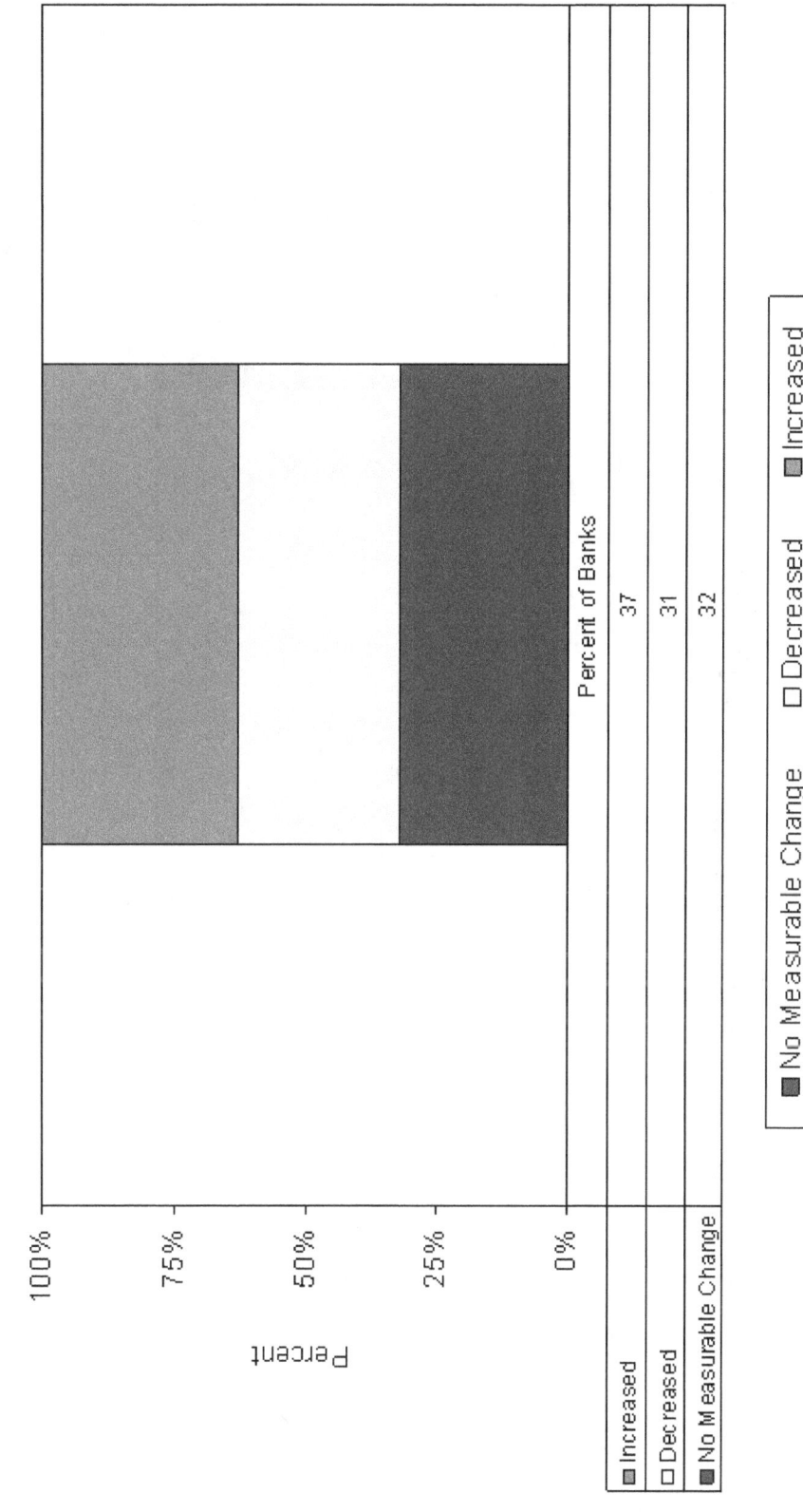

**Overall Annual Change in Loan Production**

| Percent of Banks | |
|---|---|
| Increased | 37 |
| Decreased | 31 |
| No Measurable Change | 32 |

Percent of Banks

■ No Measurable Change   □ Decreased   ■ Increased

# Sources of Loan Production Change

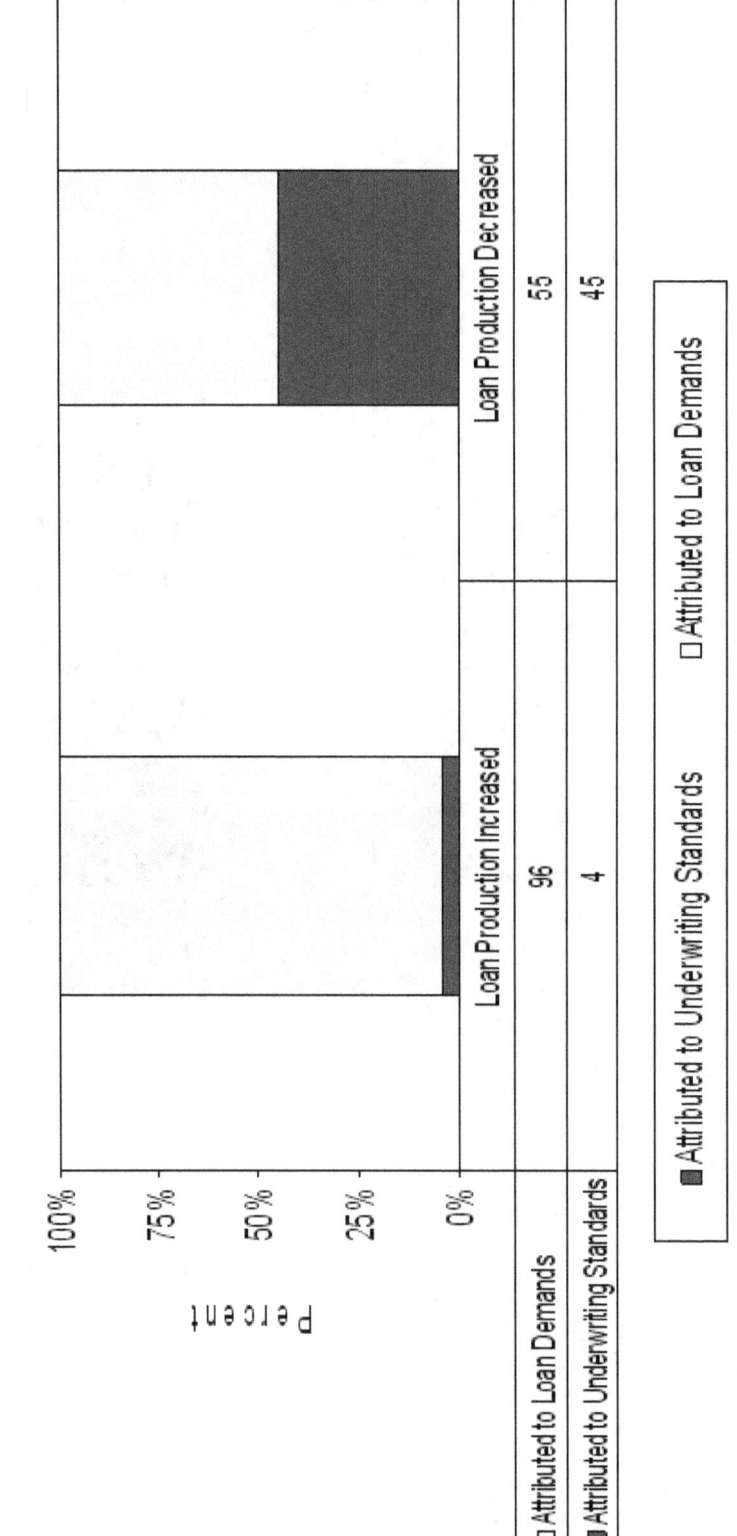

# Overall Commercial Credit Underwriting Trends

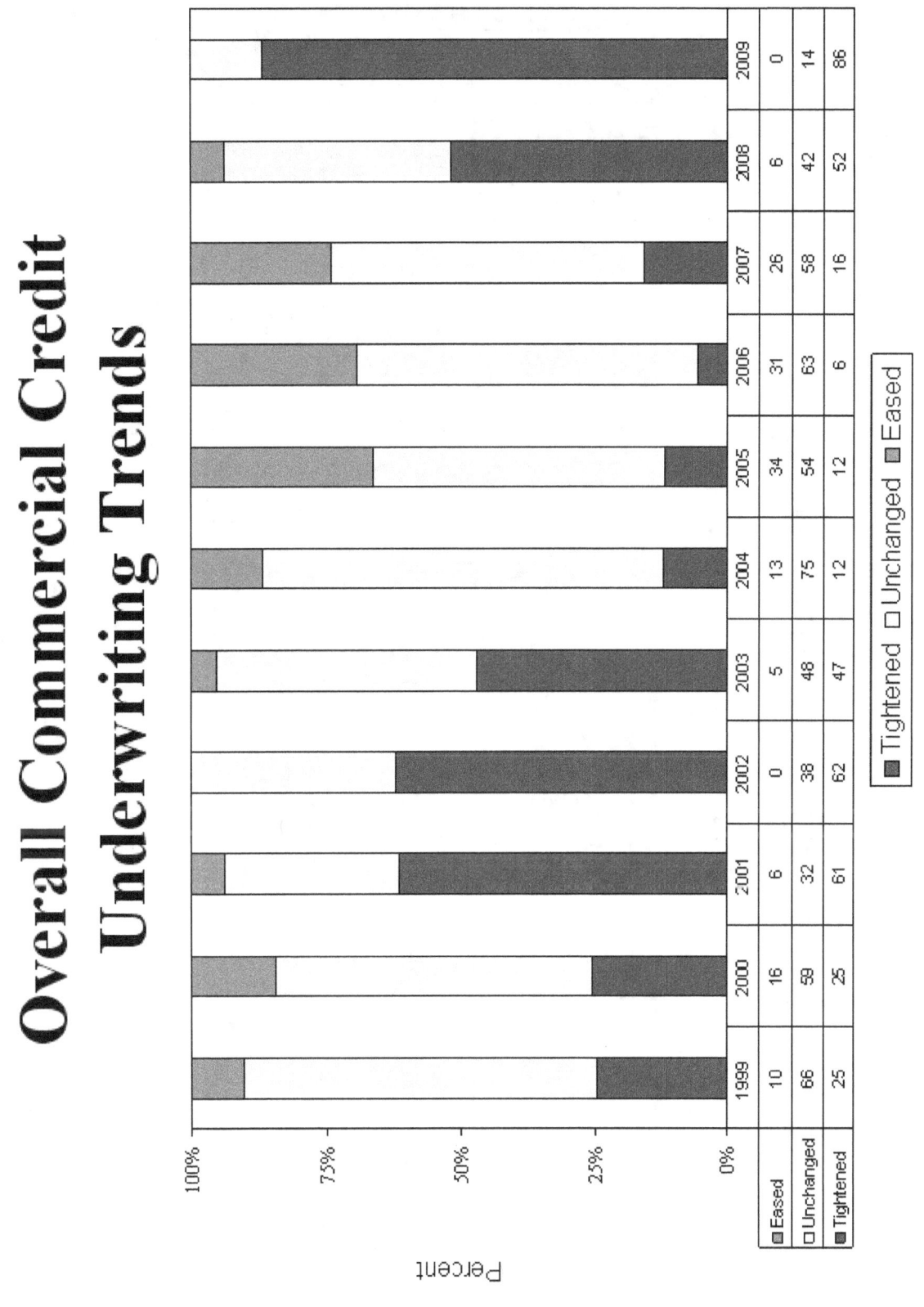

| | 1999 | 2000 | 2001 | 2002 | 2003 | 2004 | 2005 | 2006 | 2007 | 2008 | 2009 |
|---|---|---|---|---|---|---|---|---|---|---|---|
| Eased | 10 | 16 | 6 | 0 | 5 | 13 | 34 | 31 | 26 | 6 | 0 |
| Unchanged | 66 | 59 | 32 | 38 | 48 | 75 | 54 | 63 | 58 | 42 | 14 |
| Tightened | 25 | 25 | 61 | 62 | 47 | 12 | 12 | 6 | 16 | 52 | 86 |

Tightened □ Unchanged ▨ Eased

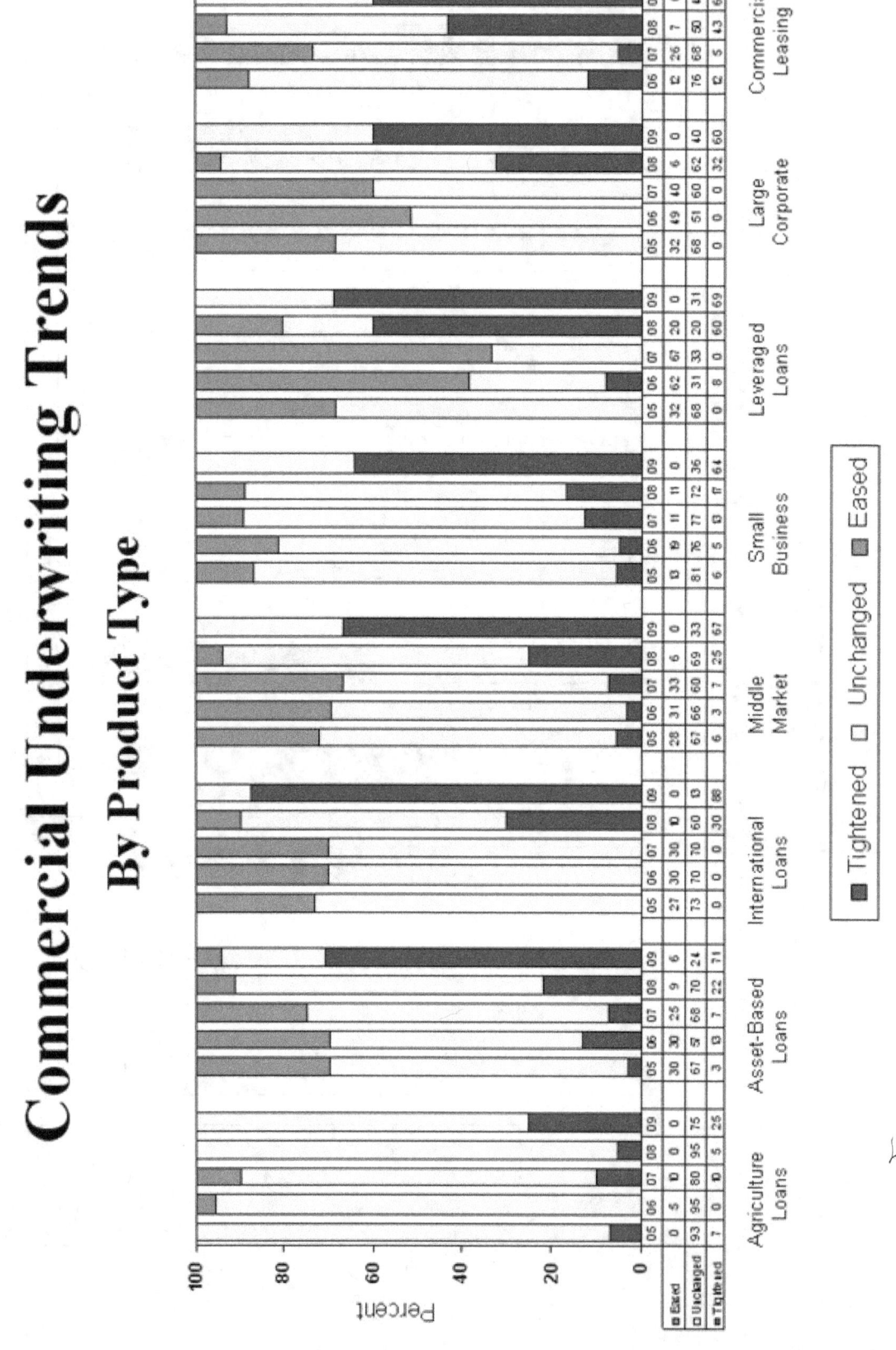

# Commercial Underwriting Trends, by Product Type (cont'd)

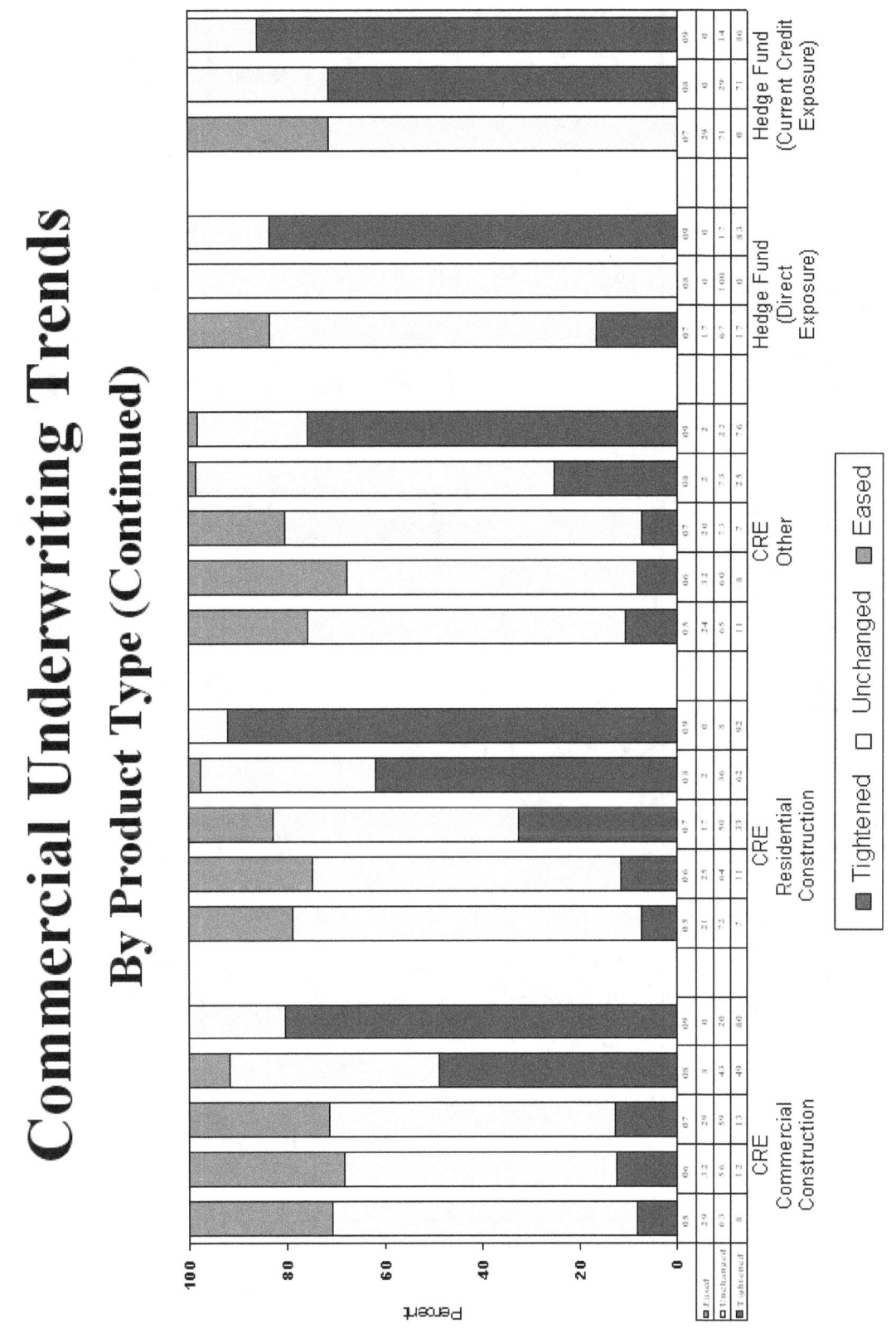

Commercial Underwriting Trends

By Product Type (Continued)

# Reasons for Tightening Commercial Underwriting Standards

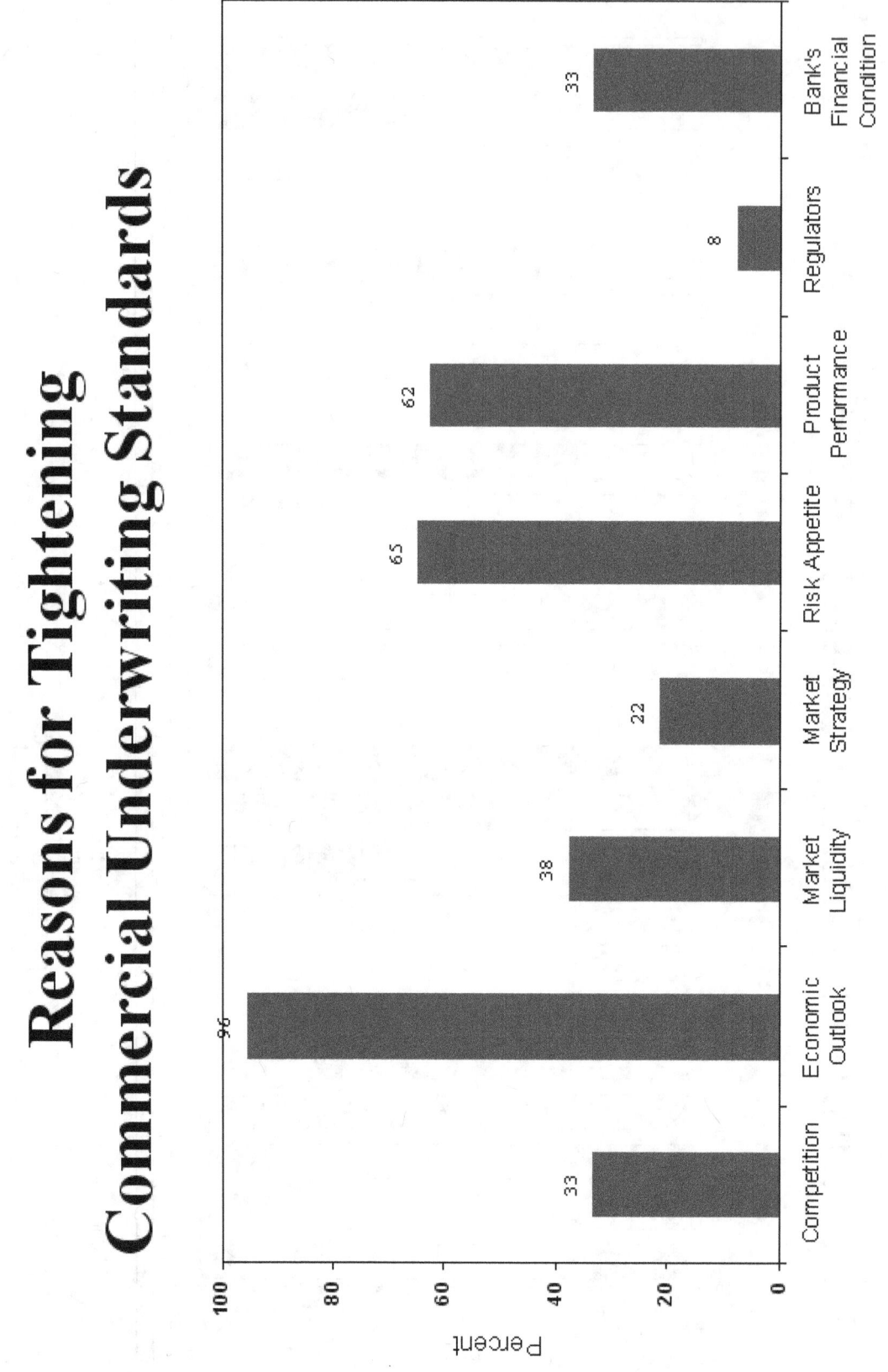

**Reasons for Tightening Commercial Underwriting Standards**

# Methods Used to Tighten Commercial Underwriting Standards

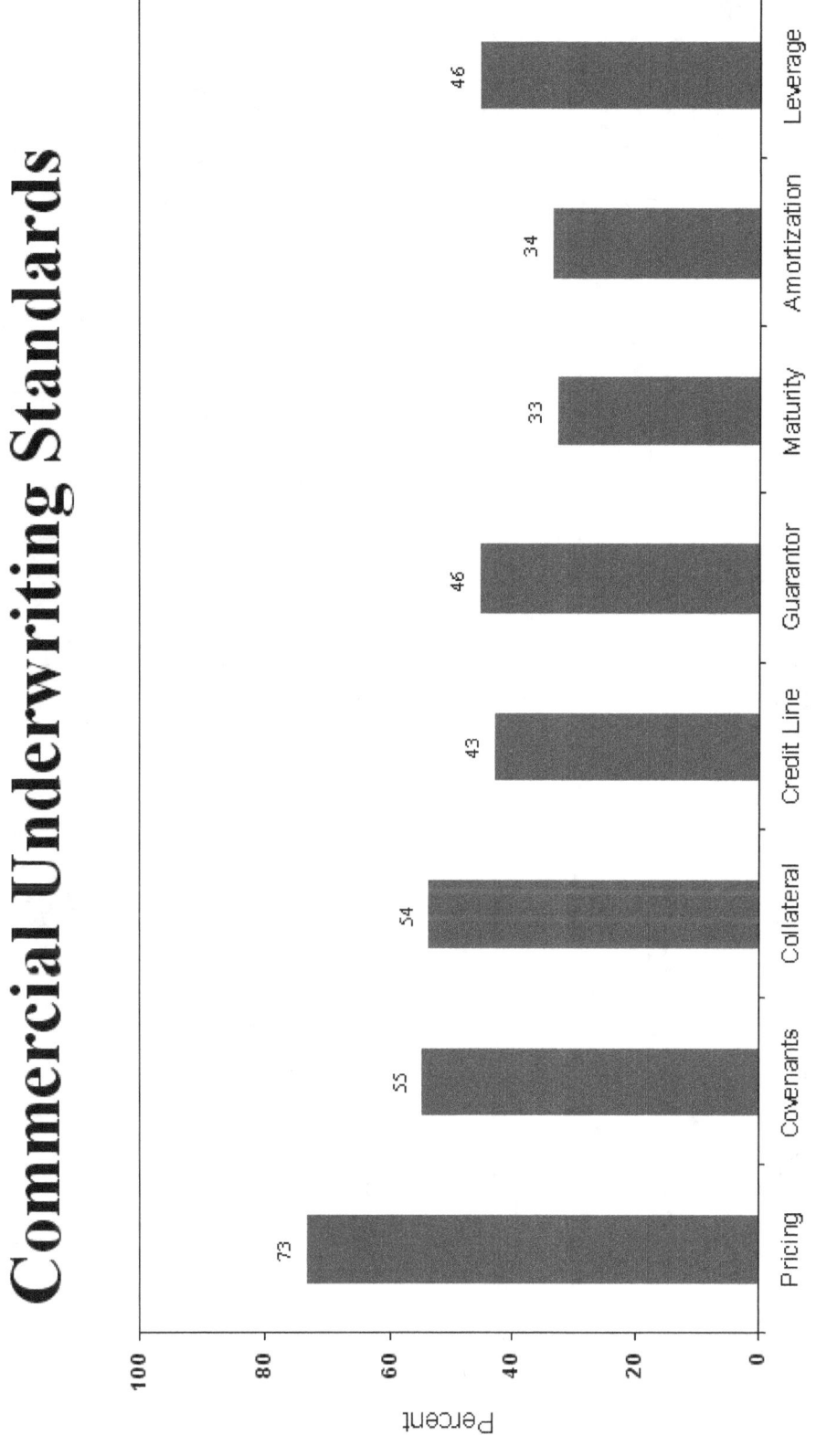

Methods Used to Tighten Commercial Underwriting Standards

| | Percent |
|---|---|
| Pricing | 73 |
| Covenants | 55 |
| Collateral | 54 |
| Credit Line | 43 |
| Guarantor | 46 |
| Maturity | 33 |
| Amortization | 34 |
| Leverage | 46 |

# Commercial Credit Risk Trends
## (Past 12 Months and Next 12 Months)

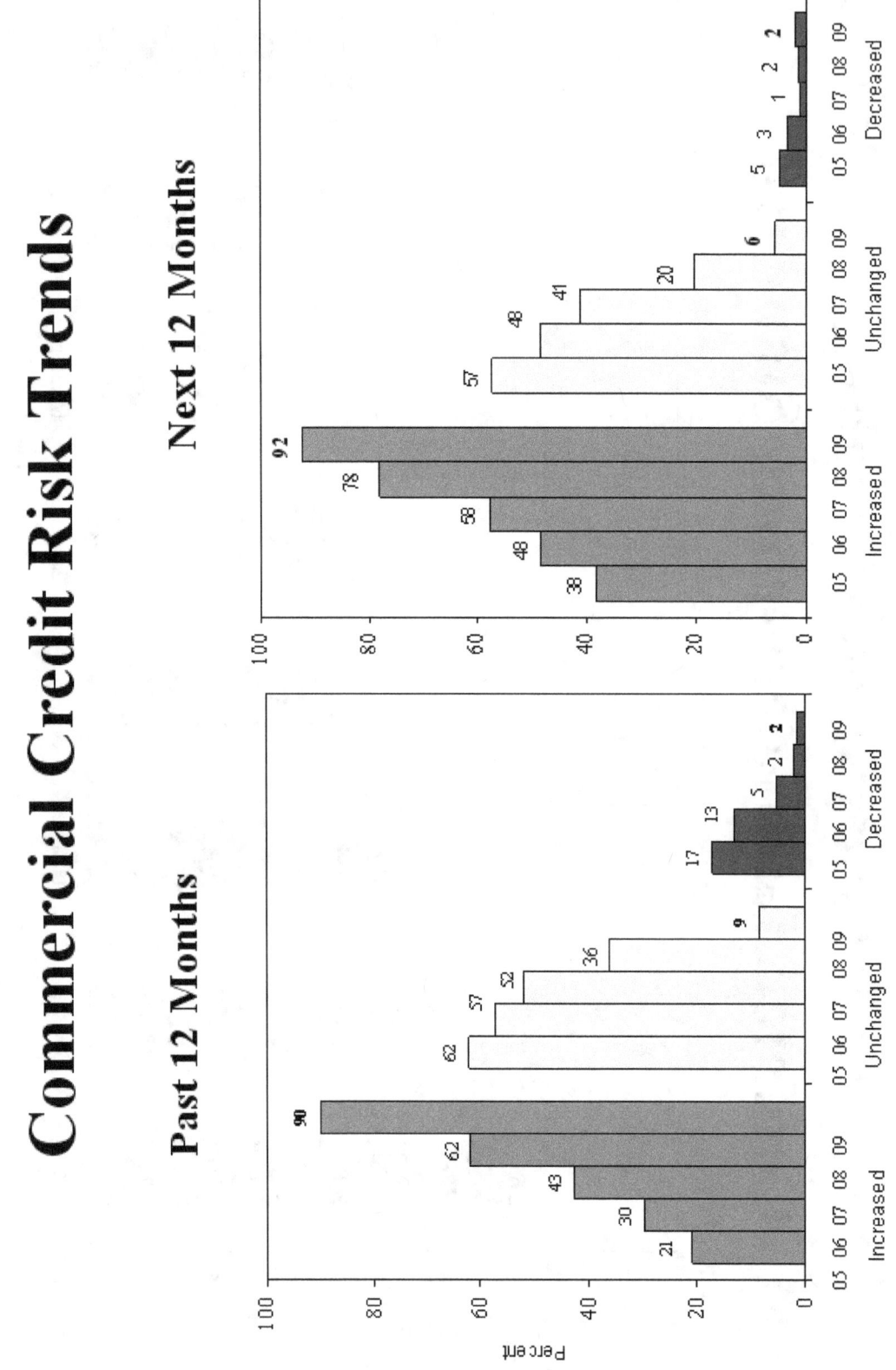

# Commercial Credit Risk Trends
## (Current Credit Risk Change, by Product Type)

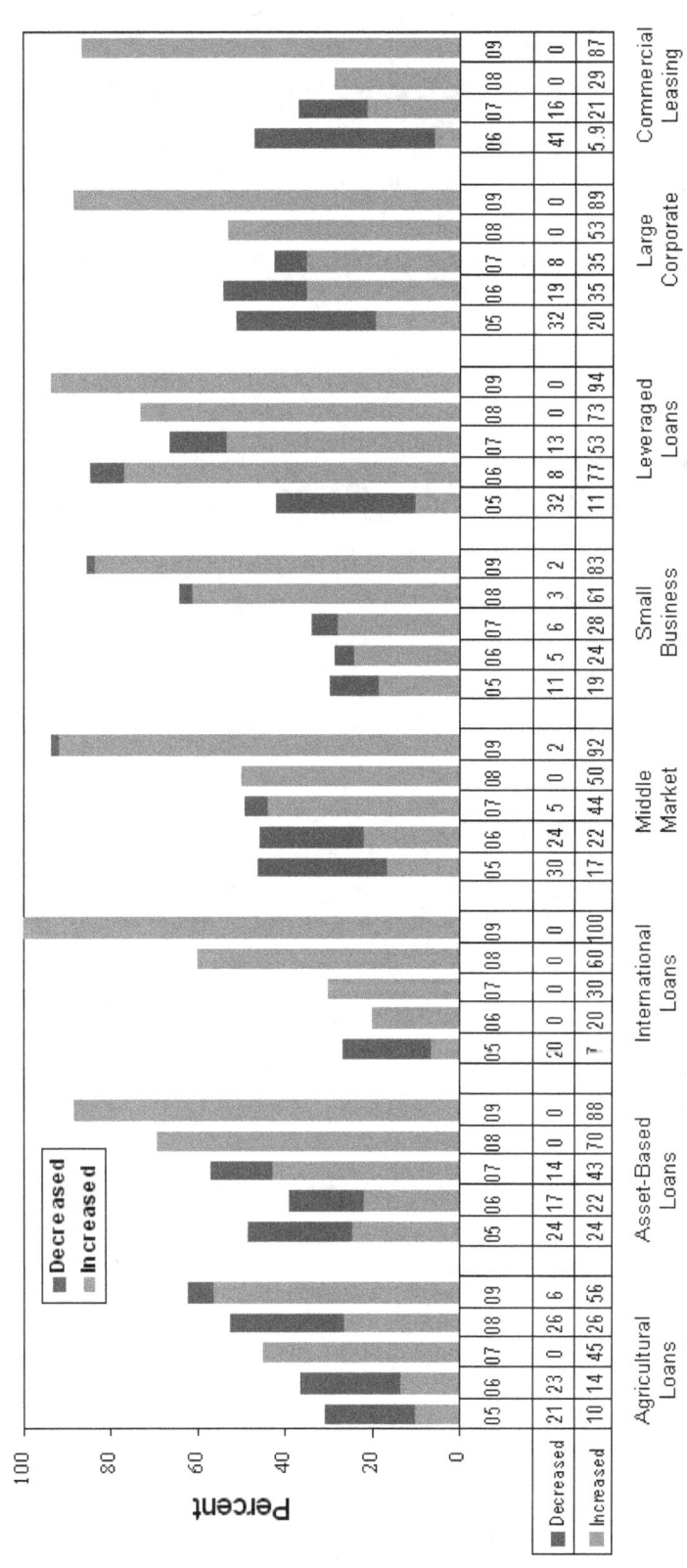

# Commercial Credit Risk Trends
## (Current Credit Risk Change, by Product Type, cont'd)

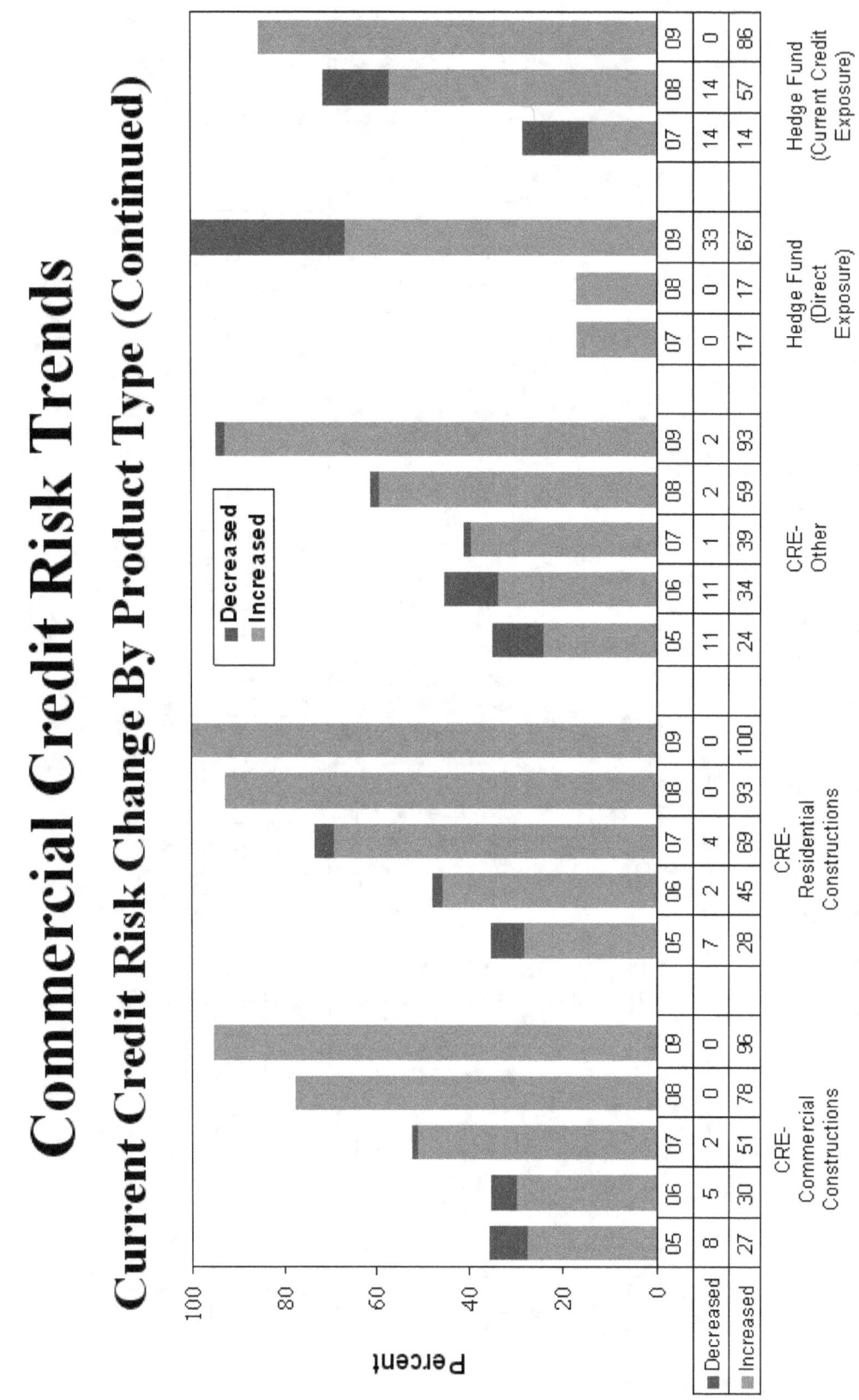

**Commercial Credit Risk Trends**

**Current Credit Risk Change By Product Type (Continued)**

Legend: ■ Decreased  ▓ Increased

| | CRE-Commercial Constructions | | | | | CRE-Residential Constructions | | | | | CRE-Other | | | | | Hedge Fund (Direct Exposure) | | | Hedge Fund (Current Credit Exposure) | | |
|---|---|---|---|---|---|---|---|---|---|---|---|---|---|---|---|---|---|---|---|---|---|---|
| | 05 | 06 | 07 | 08 | 09 | 05 | 06 | 07 | 08 | 09 | 05 | 06 | 07 | 08 | 09 | 07 | 08 | 09 | 07 | 08 | 09 |
| Decreased | 8 | 5 | 2 | 0 | 0 | 7 | 2 | 4 | 0 | 0 | 11 | 11 | 1 | 2 | 2 | 0 | 0 | 33 | 14 | 14 | 0 |
| Increased | 27 | 30 | 51 | 78 | 96 | 28 | 45 | 69 | 93 | 100 | 24 | 34 | 39 | 59 | 93 | 17 | 17 | 67 | 14 | 57 | 86 |

Percent

# Overall Retail Credit Underwriting Trends

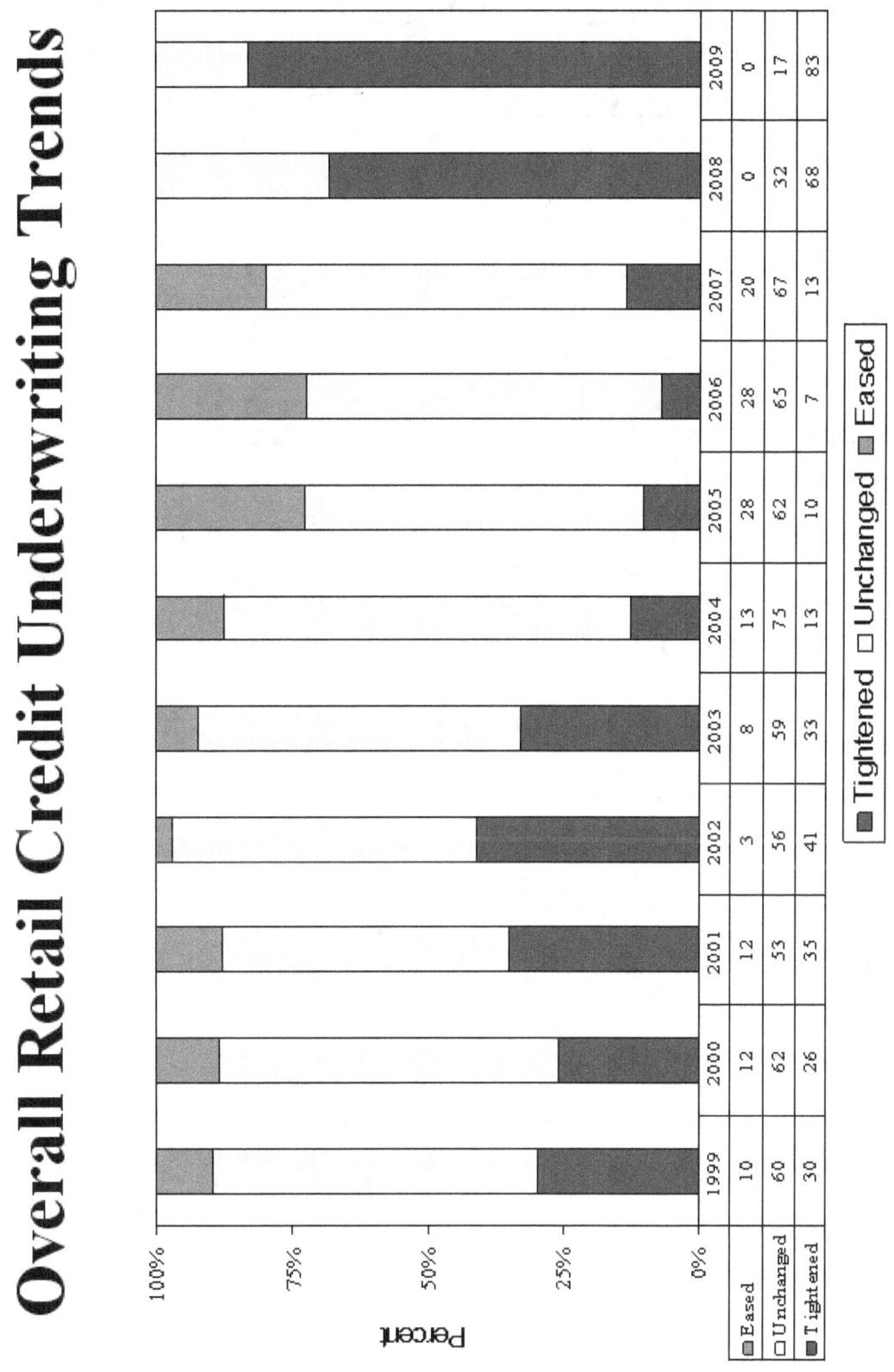

| | 1999 | 2000 | 2001 | 2002 | 2003 | 2004 | 2005 | 2006 | 2007 | 2008 | 2009 |
|---|---|---|---|---|---|---|---|---|---|---|---|
| Eased | 10 | 12 | 12 | 3 | 8 | 13 | 28 | 28 | 20 | 0 | 0 |
| Unchanged | 60 | 62 | 53 | 56 | 59 | 75 | 62 | 65 | 67 | 32 | 17 |
| Tightened | 30 | 26 | 35 | 41 | 33 | 13 | 10 | 7 | 13 | 68 | 83 |

■ Tightened  □ Unchanged  ■ Eased

# Retail Underwriting Trends, by Product Type

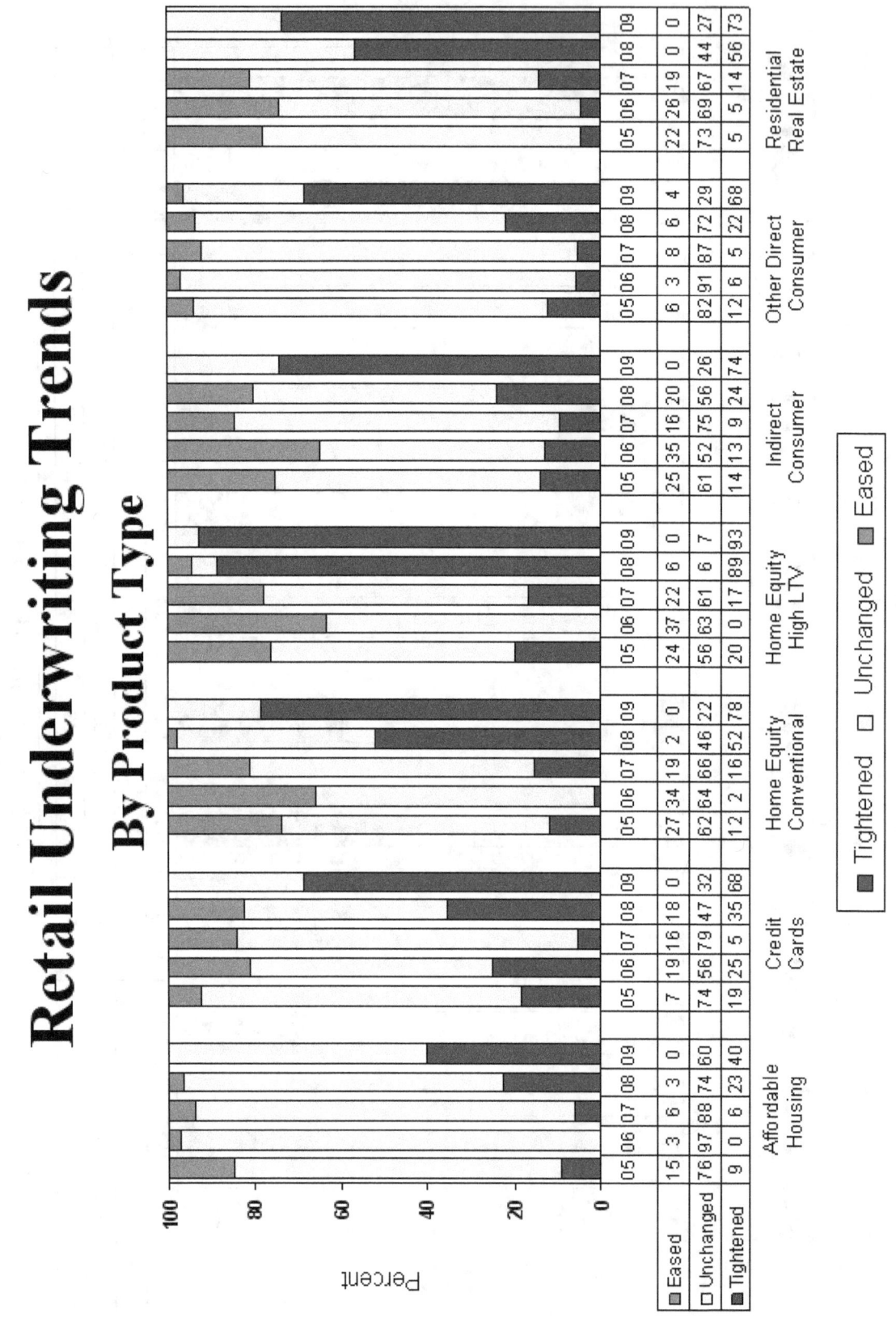

| | 05 | 06 | 07 | 08 | 09 | | 05 | 06 | 07 | 08 | 09 | | 05 | 06 | 07 | 08 | 09 | | 05 | 06 | 07 | 08 | 09 | | 05 | 06 | 07 | 08 | 09 | | 05 | 06 | 07 | 08 | 09 | | 05 | 06 | 07 | 08 | 09 |
|---|---|---|---|---|---|---|---|---|---|---|---|---|---|---|---|---|---|---|---|---|---|---|---|---|---|---|---|---|---|---|---|---|---|---|---|---|---|---|---|---|
| ■ Eased | 15 | 3 | 6 | 3 | 0 | | 7 | 19 | 16 | 18 | 0 | | 27 | 34 | 19 | 2 | 0 | | 24 | 37 | 22 | 6 | 0 | | 25 | 35 | 16 | 20 | 0 | | 6 | 3 | 8 | 6 | 4 | | 22 | 26 | 19 | 0 | 0 |
| □ Unchanged | 76 | 97 | 88 | 74 | 60 | | 74 | 56 | 79 | 47 | 32 | | 62 | 64 | 66 | 46 | 22 | | 56 | 63 | 61 | 6 | 7 | | 61 | 52 | 75 | 56 | 26 | | 82 | 91 | 87 | 72 | 29 | | 73 | 69 | 67 | 44 | 27 |
| ■ Tightened | 9 | 0 | 6 | 23 | 40 | | 19 | 25 | 5 | 35 | 68 | | 12 | 2 | 16 | 52 | 78 | | 20 | 0 | 17 | 89 | 93 | | 14 | 13 | 9 | 24 | 74 | | 12 | 6 | 5 | 22 | 68 | | 5 | 5 | 14 | 56 | 73 |
| | Affordable Housing | | | | | | Credit Cards | | | | | | Home Equity Conventional | | | | | | Home Equity High LTV | | | | | | Indirect Consumer | | | | | | Other Direct Consumer | | | | | | Residential Real Estate | | | | |

**■ Tightened □ Unchanged ■ Eased**

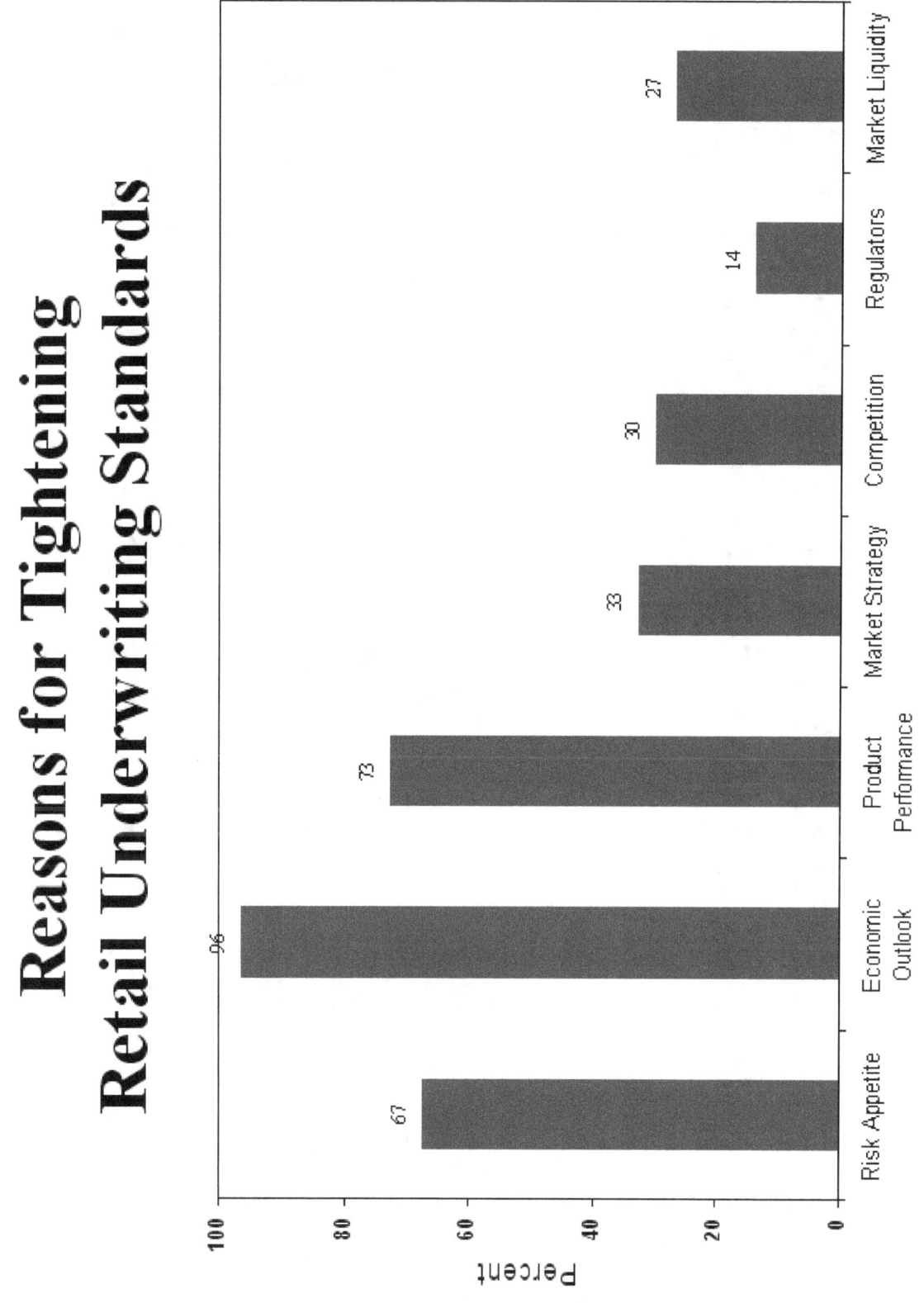

**Reasons for Tightening Retail Underwriting Standards**

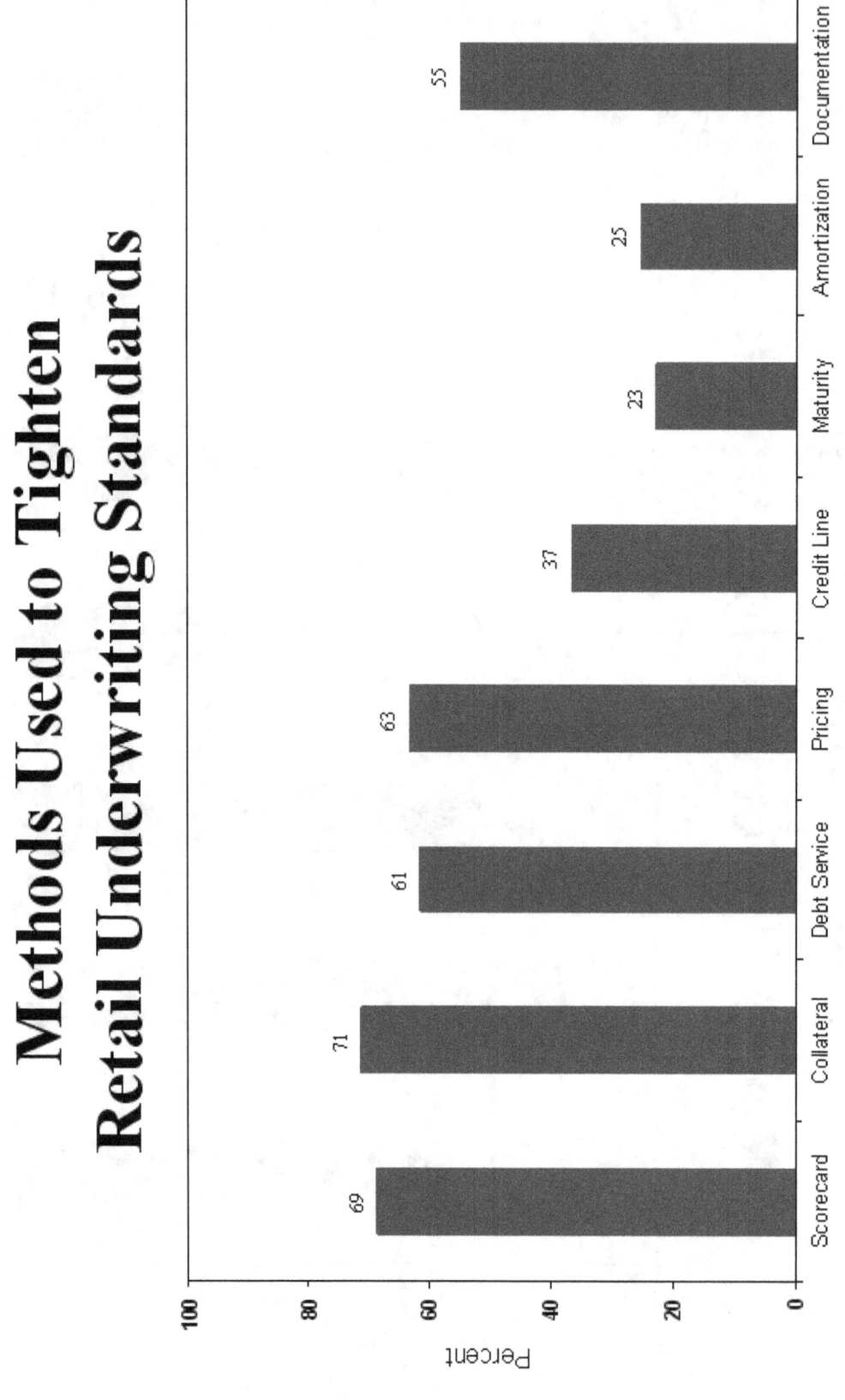

Methods Used to Tighten
Retail Underwriting Standards

# Retail Credit Risk Trends
# (Past 12 Months and Next 12 Months)

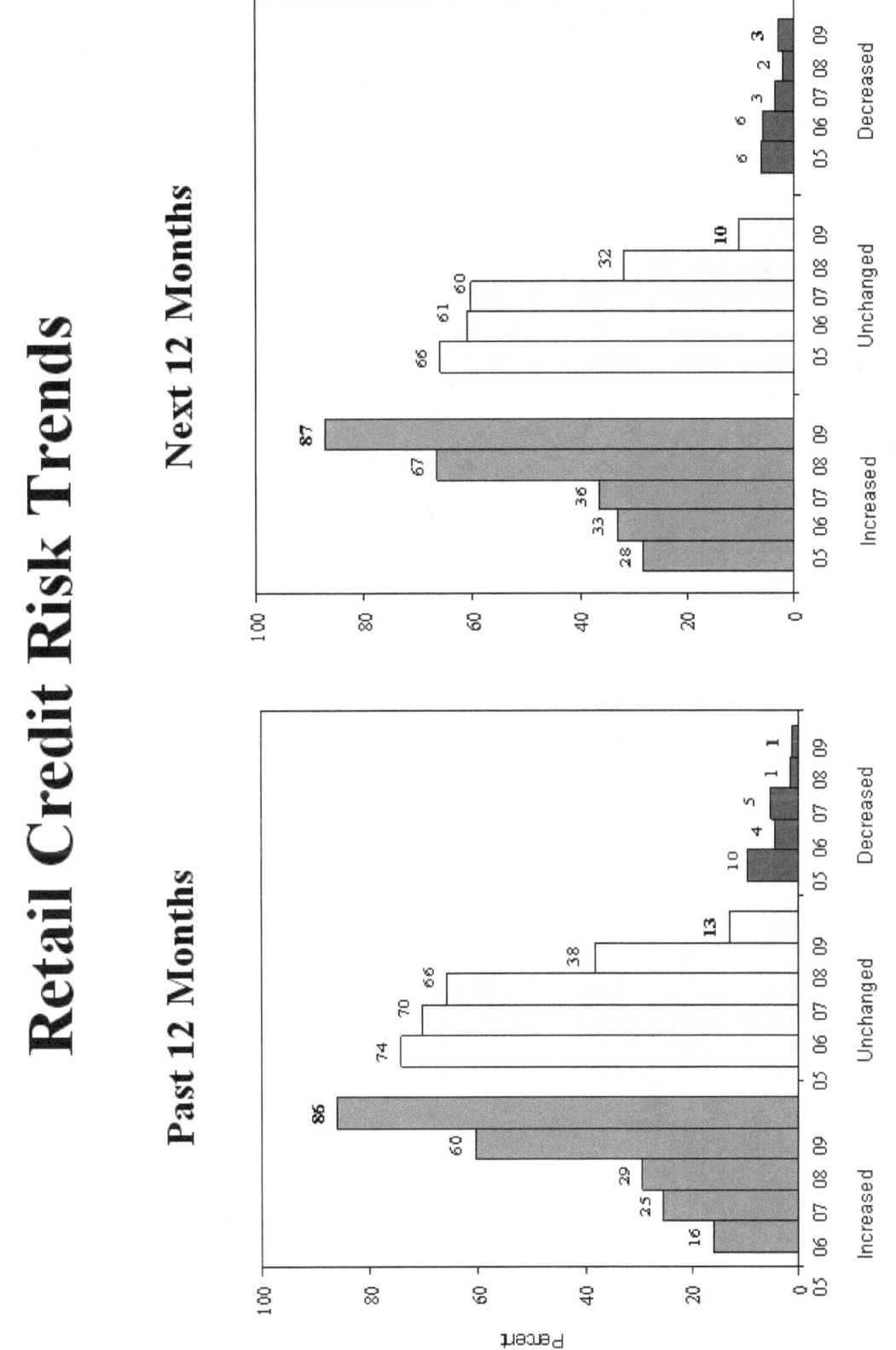

# Retail Credit Risk Trends
## (Current Credit Risk Change, by Product Type)

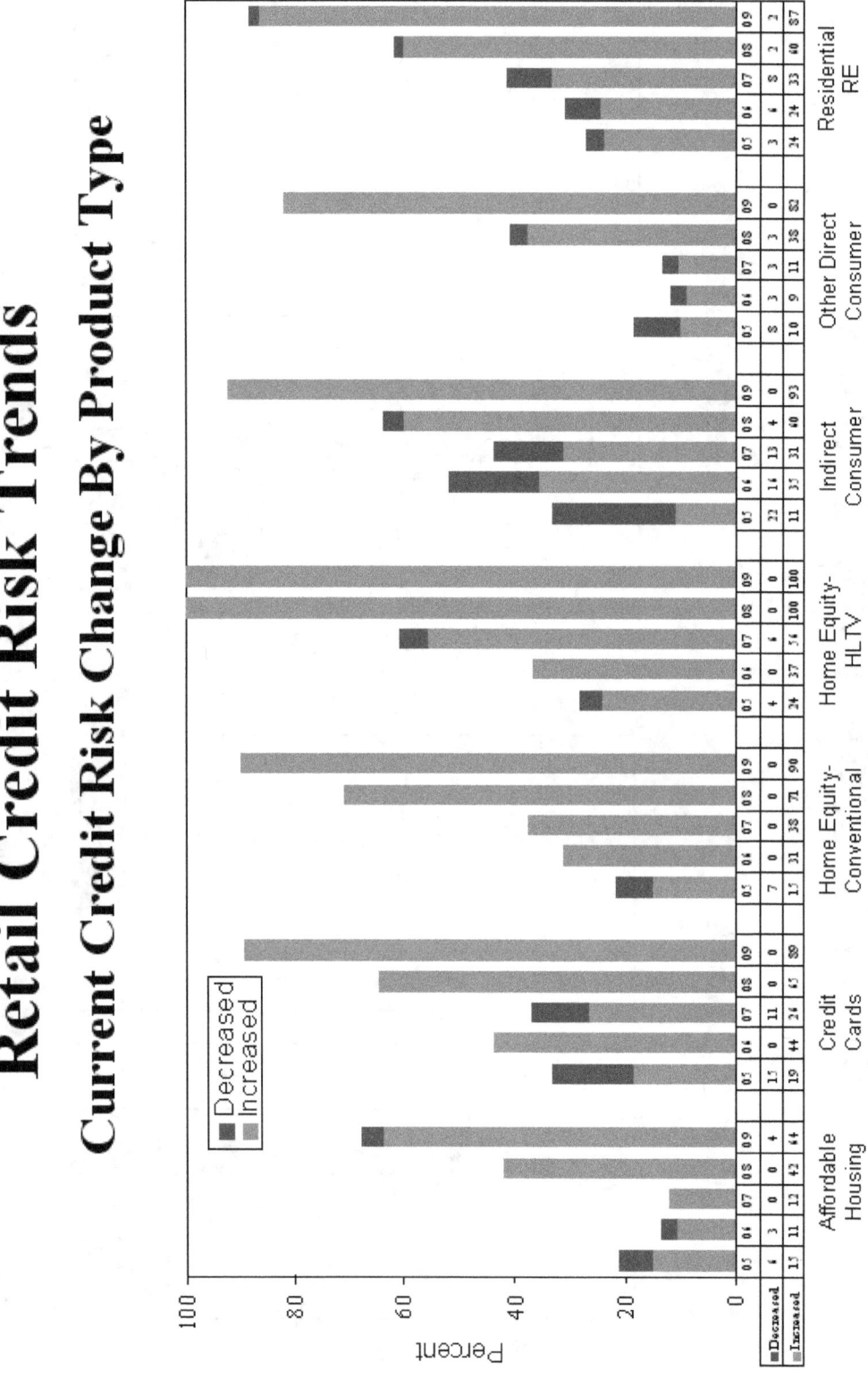

**Retail Credit Risk Trends**

**Current Credit Risk Change By Product Type**

# Origination Purpose

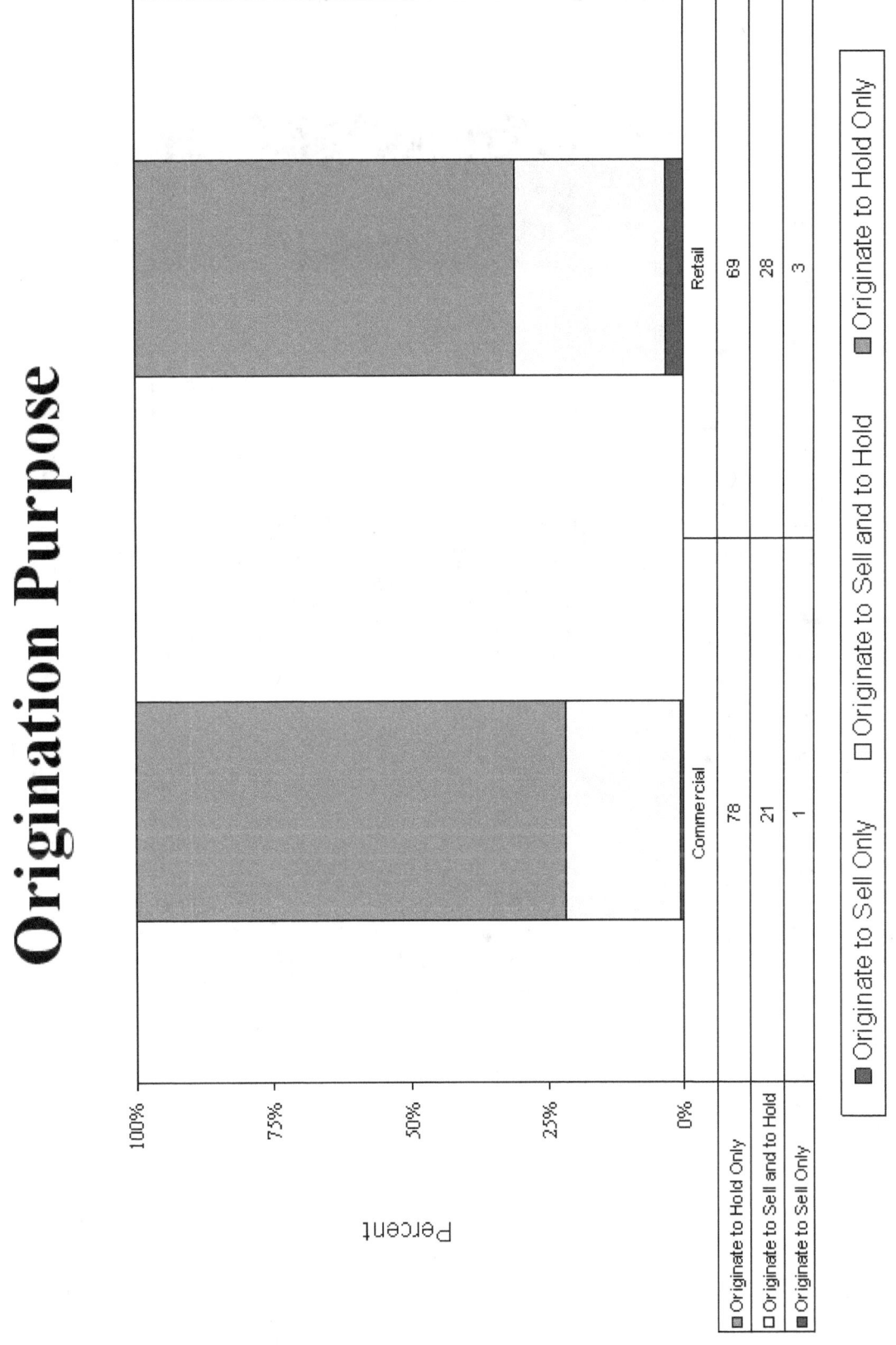

# Residential Real Estate Lending Origination Channels

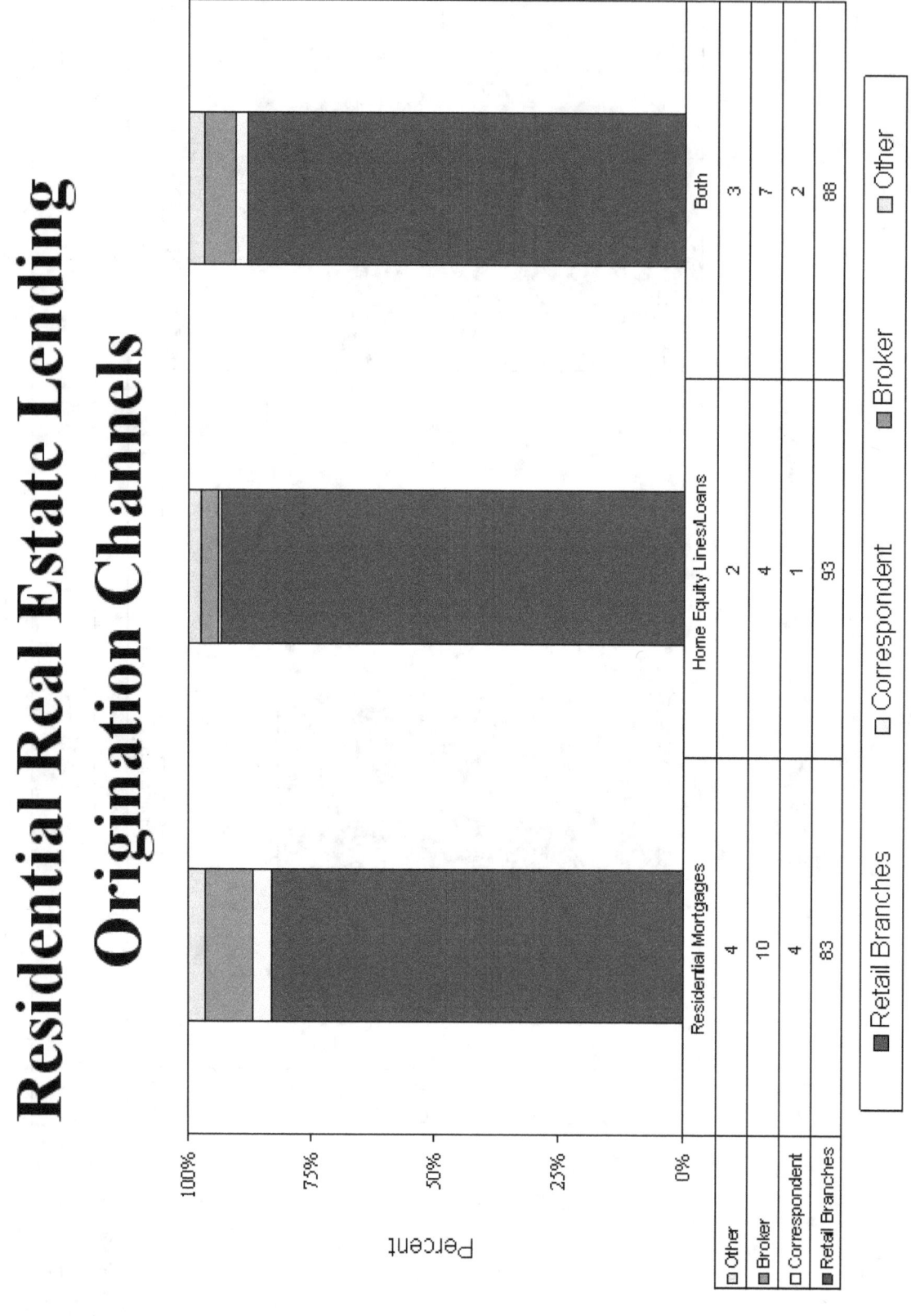

Residential Real Estate Lending Origination Channels

| | Residential Mortgages | Home Equity Lines/Loans | Both |
|---|---|---|---|
| Other | 4 | 2 | 3 |
| Broker | 10 | 4 | 7 |
| Correspondent | 4 | 1 | 2 |
| Retail Branches | 83 | 93 | 88 |

Legend: ■ Retail Branches  □ Correspondent  ■ Broker  □ Other

# Part III: Data Tables

Commercial Lending Portfolios ............................................................................. 32
    Agricultural Lending ..................................................................................... 32
    Asset-Based Loans ...................................................................................... 33
    Commercial Leasing..................................................................................... 34
    Commercial Real Estate Lending—Commercial Construction ....................... 35
    Commercial Real Estate Lending—Residential Construction ....................... 36
    Commercial Real Estate Lending—Other...................................................... 37
    International Lending .................................................................................... 38
    Middle Market Lending.................................................................................. 39
    Small Business Lending ................................................................................ 40
    Leveraged Loans .......................................................................................... 41
    Large Corporate Loans................................................................................. 42
    Hedge Funds (Direct Credit Exposure) ........................................................ 43
    Hedge Funds (Counterparty Credit Exposure) ............................................. 44
Retail Lending Portfolios ...................................................................................... 45
    Affordable Housing Lending.......................................................................... 45
    Credit Card Lending ..................................................................................... 46
    Other Direct Consumer Lending .................................................................. 47
    Home Equity—Conventional Lending............................................................ 48
    Home Equity—High LTV Lending ................................................................. 49
    Indirect Consumer Lending........................................................................... 50
    Residential Real Estate Lending................................................................... 51

# Commercial Lending Portfolios

## *Agricultural Lending*

Sixteen of the 59 banks in the survey were engaged in some form of agricultural lending.

**Changes in Underwriting Standards in Agricultural Loan Portfolios**
(Percent of Responses)

|  | Eased | Unchanged | Tightened |
|---|---|---|---|
| 2001 | 3 | 71 | 26 |
| 2002 | 0 | 70 | 30 |
| 2003 | 0 | 67 | 33 |
| 2004 | 0 | 93 | 7 |
| 2005 | 0 | 93 | 7 |
| 2006 | 5 | 95 | 0 |
| 2007 | 10 | 80 | 10 |
| 2008 | 0 | 95 | 5 |
| 2009 | 0 | 75 | 25 |

**Changes in the Level of Credit Risk in Agricultural Loan Portfolios**
(Percent of Responses)

|  | Declined Significantly | Declined Somewhat | Unchanged | Increased Somewhat | Increased Significantly |
|---|---|---|---|---|---|
| 2001 | 0 | 17 | 43 | 34 | 6 |
| 2002 | 0 | 7 | 63 | 30 | 0 |
| 2003 | 0 | 11 | 48 | 41 | 0 |
| 2004 | 0 | 10 | 59 | 31 | 0 |
| 2005 | 4 | 17 | 69 | 10 | 0 |
| 2006 | 0 | 23 | 63 | 14 | 0 |
| 2007 | 0 | 0 | 55 | 45 | 0 |
| 2008 | 0 | 26 | 47 | 26 | 0 |
| 2009 | 0 | 6 | 38 | 56 | 0 |
| Future 12 Months | 0 | 0 | 31 | 69 | 0 |

## Asset-Based Loans

Seventeen banks in the survey were engaged in asset-based lending.

### Changes in Underwriting Standards in Asset-Based Loan Portfolios
(Percent of Responses)

|  | Eased | Unchanged | Tightened |
|---|---|---|---|
| 2001 | 5 | 53 | 42 |
| 2002 | 3 | 66 | 31 |
| 2003 | 0 | 58 | 42 |
| 2004 | 16 | 71 | 13 |
| 2005 | 30 | 67 | 3 |
| 2006 | 30 | 57 | 13 |
| 2007 | 25 | 68 | 7 |
| 2008 | 9 | 70 | 22 |
| 2009 | 6 | 23 | 71 |

### Changes in the Level of Credit Risk in Asset-Based Loan Portfolios
(Percent of Responses)

|  | Declined Significantly | Declined Somewhat | Unchanged | Increased Somewhat | Increased Significantly |
|---|---|---|---|---|---|
| 2001 | 5 | 8 | 42 | 45 | 0 |
| 2002 | 0 | 0 | 50 | 50 | 0 |
| 2003 | 3 | 26 | 42 | 29 | 0 |
| 2004 | 3 | 29 | 55 | 13 | 0 |
| 2005 | 0 | 24 | 52 | 24 | 0 |
| 2006 | 0 | 17 | 61 | 22 | 0 |
| 2007 | 0 | 14 | 43 | 43 | 0 |
| 2008 | 0 | 0 | 30 | 70 | 0 |
| 2009 | 0 | 0 | 12 | 70 | 18 |
| Future 12 Months | 0 | 0 | 6 | 88 | 6 |

## Commercial Leasing

Commercial leasing was offered by 15 of the banks in the survey.

### Changes in Underwriting Standards in Commercial Leasing Portfolios
(Percent of Responses)

|      | Eased | Unchanged | Tightened |
|------|-------|-----------|-----------|
| 2006 | 12    | 76        | 12        |
| 2007 | 26    | 69        | 5         |
| 2008 | 7     | 50        | 43        |
| 2009 | 0     | 40        | 60        |

### Changes in the Level of Credit Risk in Commercial Leasing Portfolios
(Percent of Responses)

|                  | Declined Significantly | Declined Somewhat | Unchanged | Increased Somewhat | Increased Significantly |
|------------------|------------------------|-------------------|-----------|--------------------|-------------------------|
| 2006             | 6                      | 35                | 53        | 6                  | 0                       |
| 2007             | 0                      | 16                | 63        | 21                 | 0                       |
| 2008             | 0                      | 0                 | 71        | 29                 | 0                       |
| 2009             | 0                      | 0                 | 13        | 80                 | 7                       |
| Future 12 Months | 0                      | 0                 | 0         | 100                | 0                       |

## Commercial Real Estate Lending—Commercial Construction

Forty-six of the banks in the survey were engaged in commercial construction lending.

**Changes in Underwriting Standards in Commercial Construction Loan Portfolios**
(Percent of Responses)

|       | Eased | Unchanged | Tightened |
|-------|-------|-----------|-----------|
| 2003  | 2     | 61        | 37        |
| 2004  | 10    | 75        | 15        |
| 2005  | 29    | 63        | 8         |
| 2006  | 32    | 56        | 12        |
| 2007  | 28    | 59        | 13        |
| 2008  | 8     | 43        | 49        |
| 2009  | 0     | 20        | 80        |

**Changes in the Level of Credit Risk in Commercial Construction Loan Portfolios**
(Percent of Responses)

|       | Declined Significantly | Declined Somewhat | Unchanged | Increased Somewhat | Increased Significantly |
|-------|------------------------|-------------------|-----------|--------------------|-------------------------|
| 2003  | 0 | 7 | 46 | 42 | 5 |
| 2004  | 0 | 7 | 59 | 34 | 0 |
| 2005  | 2 | 5 | 65 | 28 | 0 |
| 2006  | 0 | 5 | 65 | 30 | 0 |
| 2007  | 0 | 2 | 48 | 49 | 1 |
| 2008  | 0 | 0 | 22 | 69 | 8 |
| 2009  | 0 | 0 | 5 | 54 | 41 |
| Future 12 Months | 0 | 0 | 0 | 80 | 20 |

## Commercial Real Estate Lending—Residential Construction

Thirty-eight of the banks in the survey were engaged in residential construction lending.

### Changes in Underwriting Standards in Residential Construction Loan Portfolios
(Percent of Responses)

|      | Eased | Unchanged | Tightened |
|------|-------|-----------|-----------|
| 2003 | 0 | 76 | 24 |
| 2004 | 5 | 86 | 9 |
| 2005 | 21 | 72 | 7 |
| 2006 | 25 | 64 | 11 |
| 2007 | 17 | 50 | 33 |
| 2008 | 2 | 36 | 62 |
| 2009 | 0 | 8 | 92 |

### Changes in the Level of Credit Risk in Residential Construction Loan Portfolios
(Percent of Responses)

|      | Declined Significantly | Declined Somewhat | Unchanged | Increased Somewhat | Increased Significantly |
|------|------------------------|-------------------|-----------|--------------------|-------------------------|
| 2003 | 0 | 2 | 62 | 34 | 2 |
| 2004 | 0 | 4 | 76 | 18 | 2 |
| 2005 | 2 | 6 | 65 | 27 | 0 |
| 2006 | 0 | 2 | 52 | 46 | 0 |
| 2007 | 0 | 4 | 27 | 63 | 6 |
| 2008 | 0 | 0 | 7 | 48 | 45 |
| 2009 | 0 | 0 | 0 | 34 | 66 |
| Future 12 Months | 0 | 5 | 11 | 60 | 24 |

## Commercial Real Estate Lending—Other

Fifty-eight of the banks in the survey were engaged in other commercial real estate lending.

**Changes in Underwriting Standards in Other Commercial Real Estate Loan Portfolios**
(Percent of Responses)

|       | Eased | Unchanged | Tightened |
|-------|-------|-----------|-----------|
| 2003  | 5     | 71        | 24        |
| 2004  | 8     | 83        | 9         |
| 2005  | 24    | 65        | 11        |
| 2006  | 32    | 60        | 8         |
| 2007  | 20    | 73        | 7         |
| 2008  | 2     | 73        | 25        |
| 2009  | 2     | 22        | 76        |

**Changes in the Level of Credit Risk in Other Commercial Real Estate Loan Portfolios**
(Percent of Responses)

|                  | Declined Significantly | Declined Somewhat | Unchanged | Increased Somewhat | Increased Significantly |
|------------------|------------------------|-------------------|-----------|--------------------|-------------------------|
| 2003             | 0                      | 5                 | 48        | 43                 | 4                       |
| 2004             | 0                      | 12                | 66        | 20                 | 2                       |
| 2005             | 2                      | 9                 | 65        | 24                 | 0                       |
| 2006             | 1                      | 10                | 55        | 34                 | 0                       |
| 2007             | 0                      | 2                 | 59        | 38                 | 1                       |
| 2008             | 0                      | 2                 | 39        | 58                 | 2                       |
| 2009             | 0                      | 2                 | 5         | 67                 | 26                      |
| Future 12 Months | 0                      | 0                 | 5         | 76                 | 19                      |

## International Lending

Only eight of the banks in the survey were active in international lending.

**Changes in Underwriting Standards in International Loan Portfolios**
(Percent of Responses)

|  | Eased | Unchanged | Tightened |
|---|---|---|---|
| 2001 | 29 | 57 | 14 |
| 2002 | 11 | 61 | 28 |
| 2003 | 6 | 55 | 39 |
| 2004 | 11 | 61 | 28 |
| 2005 | 27 | 73 | 0 |
| 2006 | 30 | 70 | 0 |
| 2007 | 30 | 70 | 0 |
| 2008 | 10 | 60 | 30 |
| 2009 | 0 | 13 | 87 |

**Changes in the Level of Credit Risk in International Loan Portfolios**
(Percent of Responses)

|  | Declined Significantly | Declined Somewhat | Unchanged | Increased Somewhat | Increased Significantly |
|---|---|---|---|---|---|
| 2001 | 0 | 14 | 53 | 33 | 0 |
| 2002 | 0 | 22 | 39 | 28 | 11 |
| 2003 | 0 | 6 | 55 | 33 | 6 |
| 2004 | 6 | 33 | 55 | 6 | 0 |
| 2005 | 0 | 20 | 73 | 7 | 0 |
| 2006 | 0 | 0 | 80 | 20 | 0 |
| 2007 | 0 | 0 | 70 | 30 | 0 |
| 2008 | 0 | 0 | 40 | 40 | 20 |
| 2009 | 0 | 0 | 0 | 63 | 37 |
| Future 12 Months | 0 | 0 | 0 | 63 | 37 |

## Middle Market Lending

Forty-eight of the banks in the survey were engaged in middle market lending.

### Changes in Underwriting Standards in Middle Market Loan Portfolios
(Percent of Responses)

|       | Eased | Unchanged | Tightened |
|-------|-------|-----------|-----------|
| 2001  | 11    | 48        | 41        |
| 2002  | 0     | 60        | 40        |
| 2003  | 6     | 63        | 31        |
| 2004  | 14    | 81        | 5         |
| 2005  | 28    | 67        | 5         |
| 2006  | 31    | 66        | 3         |
| 2007  | 33    | 60        | 7         |
| 2008  | 6     | 69        | 25        |
| 2009  | 0     | 33        | 67        |

### Changes in the Level of Credit Risk in Middle Market Loan Portfolios
(Percent of Responses)

|                  | Declined Significantly | Declined Somewhat | Unchanged | Increased Somewhat | Increased Significantly |
|------------------|------------------------|-------------------|-----------|--------------------|-------------------------|
| 2001             | 0                      | 2                 | 35        | 59                 | 4                       |
| 2002             | 2                      | 8                 | 22        | 66                 | 2                       |
| 2003             | 0                      | 13                | 39        | 44                 | 4                       |
| 2004             | 0                      | 28                | 52        | 18                 | 2                       |
| 2005             | 4                      | 26                | 54        | 16                 | 0                       |
| 2006             | 0                      | 24                | 54        | 20                 | 2                       |
| 2007             | 0                      | 5                 | 51        | 44                 | 0                       |
| 2008             | 0                      | 0                 | 50        | 48                 | 2                       |
| 2009             | 0                      | 2                 | 6         | 88                 | 4                       |
| Future 12 Months | 0                      | 0                 | 4         | 88                 | 8                       |

## Small Business Lending

Forty-two of the banks in the survey were lending in the small business market.

**Changes in Underwriting Standards in Small Business Loan Portfolios**
(Percent of Responses)

|  | Eased | Unchanged | Tightened |
|---|---|---|---|
| 2001 | 5 | 63 | 32 |
| 2002 | 2 | 66 | 32 |
| 2003 | 4 | 65 | 31 |
| 2004 | 11 | 74 | 15 |
| 2005 | 13 | 81 | 6 |
| 2006 | 19 | 76 | 5 |
| 2007 | 11 | 76 | 13 |
| 2008 | 11 | 72 | 17 |
| 2009 | 0 | 36 | 64 |

**Changes in the Level of Credit Risk in Small Business Loan Portfolios**
(Percent of Responses)

|  | Declined Significantly | Declined Somewhat | Unchanged | Increased Somewhat | Increased Significantly |
|---|---|---|---|---|---|
| 2001 | 0 | 3 | 60 | 37 | 0 |
| 2002 | 0 | 2 | 56 | 40 | 2 |
| 2003 | 0 | 4 | 56 | 38 | 2 |
| 2004 | 0 | 15 | 72 | 13 | 0 |
| 2005 | 0 | 11 | 70 | 19 | 0 |
| 2006 | 0 | 5 | 71 | 22 | 2 |
| 2007 | 2 | 4 | 66 | 26 | 2 |
| 2008 | 0 | 3 | 36 | 58 | 3 |
| 2009 | 0 | 2 | 14 | 72 | 12 |
| Future 12 Months | 0 | 2 | 3 | 81 | 14 |

## Leveraged Loans

Sixteen of the banks in the survey provided leveraged loans.

### Changes in Underwriting Standards in Leveraged Loan Portfolios
(Percent of Responses)

|      | Eased | Unchanged | Tightened |
|------|-------|-----------|-----------|
| 2001 | 0     | 4         | 96        |
| 2002 | 0     | 44        | 56        |
| 2003 | 0     | 48        | 52        |
| 2004 | 15    | 85        | 0         |
| 2005 | 32    | 68        | 0         |
| 2006 | 61    | 31        | 8         |
| 2007 | 67    | 33        | 0         |
| 2008 | 20    | 20        | 60        |
| 2009 | 0     | 31        | 69        |

### Changes in the Level of Credit Risk in Leveraged Loan Portfolios
(Percent of Responses)

|      | Declined Significantly | Declined Somewhat | Unchanged | Increased Somewhat | Increased Significantly |
|------|------------------------|-------------------|-----------|--------------------|-------------------------|
| 2001 | 0  | 4  | 8  | 46 | 42 |
| 2002 | 0  | 7  | 26 | 52 | 15 |
| 2003 | 10 | 33 | 28 | 29 | 0  |
| 2004 | 15 | 40 | 40 | 5  | 0  |
| 2005 | 5  | 27 | 58 | 5  | 5  |
| 2006 | 0  | 8  | 15 | 69 | 8  |
| 2007 | 0  | 13 | 34 | 53 | 0  |
| 2008 | 0  | 0  | 27 | 53 | 20 |
| 2009 | 0  | 0  | 6  | 63 | 31 |
| Future 12 Months | 0 | 0 | 6 | 69 | 25 |

## Large Corporate Loans

Thirty-five of the banks in the survey were active in the large corporate loan market.

### Changes in Underwriting Standards in Large Corporate Loan Portfolios
(Percent of Responses)

|  | Eased | Unchanged | Tightened |
|---|---|---|---|
| 2001 | 0 | 34 | 66 |
| 2002 | 0 | 45 | 55 |
| 2003 | 3 | 49 | 48 |
| 2004 | 17 | 66 | 17 |
| 2005 | 32 | 68 | 0 |
| 2006 | 49 | 51 | 0 |
| 2007 | 40 | 60 | 0 |
| 2008 | 6 | 62 | 32 |
| 2009 | 0 | 40 | 60 |

### Changes in the Level of Credit Risk in Large Corporate Loan Portfolios
(Percent of Responses)

|  | Declined Significantly | Declined Somewhat | Unchanged | Increased Somewhat | Increased Significantly |
|---|---|---|---|---|---|
| 2001 | 0 | 6 | 17 | 63 | 14 |
| 2002 | 0 | 8 | 29 | 53 | 10 |
| 2003 | 5 | 27 | 33 | 30 | 5 |
| 2004 | 17 | 36 | 36 | 11 | 0 |
| 2005 | 5 | 27 | 49 | 19 | 0 |
| 2006 | 0 | 19 | 46 | 32 | 3 |
| 2007 | 0 | 8 | 57 | 35 | 0 |
| 2008 | 0 | 0 | 47 | 47 | 6 |
| 2009 | 0 | 0 | 12 | 77 | 11 |
| Future 12 Months | 0 | 0 | 3 | 89 | 8 |

## Hedge Funds (Direct Credit Exposure)

Only six of the banks in the survey were active in direct lending to hedge funds.

### Changes in Underwriting Standards in Hedge Funds (Direct Credit Exposure)
(Percent of Responses)

|  | Eased | Unchanged | Tightened |
|---|---|---|---|
| 2007 | 17 | 66 | 17 |
| 2008 | 0 | 100 | 0 |
| 2009 | 0 | 17 | 83 |

### Changes in the Level of Credit Risk in Hedge Funds (Direct Credit Exposure)
(Percent of Responses)

|  | Declined Significantly | Declined Somewhat | Unchanged | Increased Somewhat | Increased Significantly |
|---|---|---|---|---|---|
| 2007 | 0 | 0 | 83 | 17 | 0 |
| 2008 | 0 | 0 | 83 | 17 | 0 |
| 2009 | 33 | 0 | 0 | 34 | 33 |
| Future 12 Months | 17 | 33 | 0 | 33 | 17 |

## Hedge Funds (Counterparty Credit Exposure)

Only seven of the banks in the survey had sizable counterparty credit exposures to hedge funds.

**Changes in Underwriting Standards in Hedge Funds (Counterparty Credit Exposure)**
(Percent of Responses)

|      | Eased | Unchanged | Tightened |
|------|-------|-----------|-----------|
| 2007 | 29    | 71        | 0         |
| 2008 | 0     | 29        | 71        |
| 2009 | 0     | 14        | 86        |

**Changes in the Level of Credit Risk in Hedge Funds (Counterparty Credit Exposure)**
(Percent of Responses)

|                 | Declined Significantly | Declined Somewhat | Unchanged | Increased Somewhat | Increased Significantly |
|-----------------|------------------------|-------------------|-----------|--------------------|-------------------------|
| 2007            | 0                      | 14                | 72        | 14                 | 0                       |
| 2008            | 0                      | 14                | 29        | 43                 | 14                      |
| 2009            | 0                      | 0                 | 14        | 57                 | 29                      |
| Future 12 Months | 0                     | 14                | 29        | 57                 | 0                       |

# Retail Lending Portfolios

## Affordable Housing Lending

Twenty-five of the banks in the survey were reported to have made affordable housing loans.

**Changes in Underwriting Standards in Affordable Housing Loan Portfolios**
(Percent of Responses)

| | Eased | Unchanged | Tightened |
|---|---|---|---|
| 2001 | 6 | 88 | 6 |
| 2002 | 3 | 91 | 6 |
| 2003 | 3 | 88 | 9 |
| 2004 | 6 | 86 | 8 |
| 2005 | 15 | 76 | 9 |
| 2006 | 3 | 97 | 0 |
| 2007 | 6 | 88 | 6 |
| 2008 | 3 | 74 | 23 |
| 2009 | 0 | 60 | 40 |

**Changes in the Level of Credit Risk in Affordable Housing Loan Portfolios**
(Percent of Responses)

| | Declined Significantly | Declined Somewhat | Unchanged | Increased Somewhat | Increased Significantly |
|---|---|---|---|---|---|
| 2001 | 2 | 2 | 88 | 8 | 0 |
| 2002 | 0 | 6 | 73 | 21 | 0 |
| 2003 | 0 | 9 | 76 | 15 | 0 |
| 2004 | 0 | 9 | 82 | 9 | 0 |
| 2005 | 0 | 6 | 79 | 15 | 0 |
| 2006 | 0 | 3 | 86 | 11 | 0 |
| 2007 | 0 | 0 | 88 | 12 | 0 |
| 2008 | 0 | 0 | 58 | 35 | 6 |
| 2009 | 0 | 4 | 32 | 52 | 12 |
| Future 12 Months | 0 | 0 | 28 | 60 | 12 |

## Credit Card Lending

Nineteen of the banks in the survey were engaged in credit card lending.

### Changes in Underwriting Standards in Credit Card Loan Portfolios
(Percent of Responses)

|  | Eased | Unchanged | Tightened |
|---|---|---|---|
| 2001 | 16 | 60 | 24 |
| 2002 | 12 | 66 | 22 |
| 2003 | 19 | 62 | 19 |
| 2004 | 18 | 61 | 21 |
| 2005 | 7 | 74 | 19 |
| 2006 | 19 | 56 | 25 |
| 2007 | 16 | 79 | 5 |
| 2008 | 18 | 47 | 35 |
| 2009 | 0 | 32 | 68 |

### Changes in the Level of Credit Risk in Credit Card Loan Portfolios
(Percent of Responses)

|  | Declined Significantly | Declined Somewhat | Unchanged | Increased Somewhat | Increased Significantly |
|---|---|---|---|---|---|
| 2001 | 8 | 5 | 57 | 27 | 3 |
| 2002 | 0 | 6 | 54 | 31 | 9 |
| 2003 | 0 | 22 | 48 | 30 | 0 |
| 2004 | 0 | 11 | 61 | 25 | 3 |
| 2005 | 0 | 15 | 67 | 18 | 0 |
| 2006 | 0 | 0 | 56 | 44 | 0 |
| 2007 | 0 | 11 | 63 | 26 | 0 |
| 2008 | 0 | 0 | 35 | 65 | 0 |
| 2009 | 0 | 0 | 10 | 53 | 37 |
| Future 12 Months | 0 | 0 | 5 | 69 | 26 |

## Other Direct Consumer Lending

Twenty-eight of the banks in the survey were engaged in other direct consumer lending.

### Changes in Underwriting Standards in Other Direct Consumer Loan Portfolios
(Percent of Responses)

|  | Eased | Unchanged | Tightened |
|------|------|------|------|
| 2001 | 7 | 73 | 20 |
| 2002 | 2 | 67 | 31 |
| 2003 | 8 | 68 | 24 |
| 2004 | 3 | 86 | 11 |
| 2005 | 6 | 82 | 12 |
| 2006 | 3 | 91 | 6 |
| 2007 | 8 | 87 | 5 |
| 2008 | 6 | 72 | 22 |
| 2009 | 4 | 28 | 68 |

### Changes in the Level of Credit Risk in Other Direct Consumer Loan Portfolios
(Percent of Responses)

|  | Declined Significantly | Declined Somewhat | Unchanged | Increased Somewhat | Increased Significantly |
|------|------|------|------|------|------|
| 2001 | 0 | 7 | 71 | 20 | 2 |
| 2002 | 2 | 6 | 67 | 25 | 0 |
| 2003 | 2 | 17 | 72 | 7 | 2 |
| 2004 | 2 | 13 | 78 | 7 | 0 |
| 2005 | 0 | 8 | 82 | 10 | 0 |
| 2006 | 0 | 3 | 88 | 9 | 0 |
| 2007 | 0 | 3 | 87 | 10 | 0 |
| 2008 | 0 | 3 | 59 | 38 | 0 |
| 2009 | 0 | 0 | 18 | 68 | 14 |
| Future 12 Months | 0 | 0 | 11 | 78 | 11 |

## Home Equity—Conventional Lending

Fifty-one of the banks in the survey offered the conventional home equity lending product.

### Changes in Underwriting Standards in Home Equity—Conventional Loan Portfolios
(Percent of Responses)

|  | Eased | Unchanged | Tightened |
|---|---|---|---|
| 2001 | 7 | 70 | 23 |
| 2002 | 0 | 74 | 26 |
| 2003 | 18 | 63 | 19 |
| 2004 | 13 | 77 | 10 |
| 2005 | 27 | 62 | 11 |
| 2006 | 34 | 64 | 2 |
| 2007 | 19 | 65 | 16 |
| 2008 | 2 | 46 | 52 |
| 2009 | 0 | 22 | 78 |

### Changes in the Level of Credit Risk in Home Equity—Conventional Loan Portfolios
(Percent of Responses)

|  | Declined Significantly | Declined Somewhat | Unchanged | Increased Somewhat | Increased Significantly |
|---|---|---|---|---|---|
| 2001 | 0 | 11 | 74 | 13 | 2 |
| 2002 | 0 | 7 | 71 | 22 | 0 |
| 2003 | 4 | 4 | 69 | 23 | 0 |
| 2004 | 0 | 6 | 79 | 13 | 2 |
| 2005 | 0 | 7 | 78 | 15 | 0 |
| 2006 | 0 | 0 | 69 | 29 | 2 |
| 2007 | 0 | 0 | 63 | 34 | 3 |
| 2008 | 0 | 0 | 29 | 52 | 19 |
| 2009 | 0 | 0 | 10 | 63 | 27 |
| Future 12 Months | 0 | 2 | 4 | 80 | 14 |

## Home Equity—High LTV Lending

Fourteen of the banks in the survey offered the high LTV home equity lending product.

**Changes in Underwriting Standards in Home Equity—High LTV Loan Portfolios**
(Percent of Responses)

|  | Eased | Unchanged | Tightened |
|---|---|---|---|
| 2001 | 11 | 54 | 35 |
| 2002 | 0 | 56 | 44 |
| 2003 | 7 | 68 | 25 |
| 2004 | 18 | 71 | 11 |
| 2005 | 24 | 56 | 20 |
| 2006 | 37 | 63 | 0 |
| 2007 | 22 | 61 | 17 |
| 2008 | 6 | 6 | 89 |
| 2009 | 0 | 7 | 93 |

**Changes in the Level of Credit Risk in Home Equity—High LTV Loan Portfolios**
(Percent of Responses)

|  | Declined Significantly | Declined Somewhat | Unchanged | Increased Somewhat | Increased Significantly |
|---|---|---|---|---|---|
| 2001 | 5 | 11 | 62 | 16 | 6 |
| 2002 | 0 | 12 | 40 | 44 | 4 |
| 2003 | 0 | 11 | 50 | 36 | 3 |
| 2004 | 0 | 18 | 61 | 18 | 3 |
| 2005 | 0 | 4 | 72 | 24 | 0 |
| 2006 | 0 | 0 | 63 | 37 | 0 |
| 2007 | 0 | 6 | 39 | 55 | 0 |
| 2008 | 0 | 0 | 0 | 56 | 44 |
| 2009 | 0 | 0 | 0 | 36 | 64 |
| Future 12 Months | 0 | 7 | 0 | 57 | 36 |

## Indirect Consumer Lending

Twenty-seven of the banks in the survey were engaged in indirect consumer lending.

**Changes in Underwriting Standards in Indirect Consumer Loan Portfolios**
(Percent of Responses)

|      | Eased | Unchanged | Tightened |
|------|-------|-----------|-----------|
| 2001 | 7     | 63        | 30        |
| 2002 | 0     | 72        | 28        |
| 2003 | 5     | 65        | 30        |
| 2004 | 11    | 60        | 29        |
| 2005 | 25    | 61        | 14        |
| 2006 | 35    | 52        | 13        |
| 2007 | 16    | 75        | 9         |
| 2008 | 20    | 56        | 24        |
| 2009 | 0     | 26        | 74        |

**Changes in the Level of Credit Risk in Indirect Consumer Loan Portfolios**
(Percent of Responses)

|                  | Declined Significantly | Declined Somewhat | Unchanged | Increased Somewhat | Increased Significantly |
|------------------|------------------------|-------------------|-----------|--------------------|-------------------------|
| 2001             | 2                      | 21                | 39        | 33                 | 5                       |
| 2002             | 3                      | 13                | 38        | 43                 | 3                       |
| 2003             | 5                      | 20                | 47        | 28                 | 0                       |
| 2004             | 0                      | 26                | 60        | 14                 | 0                       |
| 2005             | 3                      | 19                | 67        | 8                  | 3                       |
| 2006             | 6                      | 10                | 48        | 36                 | 0                       |
| 2007             | 0                      | 3                 | 87        | 10                 | 0                       |
| 2008             | 0                      | 4                 | 36        | 60                 | 0                       |
| 2009             | 0                      | 0                 | 7         | 74                 | 19                      |
| Future 12 Months | 0                      | 11                | 15        | 63                 | 11                      |

## Residential Real Estate Lending

Fifty-two of the banks in the survey were engaged in residential real estate lending.

**Changes in Underwriting Standards in Residential Real Estate Loan Portfolios**
(Percent of Responses)

|      | Eased | Unchanged | Tightened |
|------|-------|-----------|-----------|
| 2001 | 12    | 72        | 16        |
| 2002 | 4     | 83        | 13        |
| 2003 | 2     | 86        | 12        |
| 2004 | 7     | 86        | 7         |
| 2005 | 22    | 73        | 5         |
| 2006 | 26    | 69        | 5         |
| 2007 | 19    | 67        | 14        |
| 2008 | 0     | 44        | 56        |
| 2009 | 0     | 27        | 73        |

**Changes in the Level of Credit Risk in Residential Real Estate Loan Portfolios**
(Percent of Responses)

|                  | Declined Significantly | Declined Somewhat | Unchanged | Increased Somewhat | Increased Significantly |
|------------------|------------------------|-------------------|-----------|--------------------|-------------------------|
| 2001             | 0                      | 9                 | 76        | 15                 | 0                       |
| 2002             | 0                      | 8                 | 68        | 24                 | 0                       |
| 2003             | 0                      | 12                | 74        | 12                 | 2                       |
| 2004             | 0                      | 6                 | 92        | 2                  | 0                       |
| 2005             | 0                      | 3                 | 73        | 24                 | 0                       |
| 2006             | 0                      | 7                 | 69        | 24                 | 0                       |
| 2007             | 2                      | 6                 | 59        | 33                 | 0                       |
| 2008             | 2                      | 0                 | 38        | 55                 | 5                       |
| 2009             | 0                      | 2                 | 12        | 69                 | 17                      |
| Future 12 Months | 0                      | 2                 | 10        | 77                 | 11                      |

www.ingramcontent.com/pod-product-compliance
Lightning Source LLC
Chambersburg PA
CBHW080608290526
45790CB00007B/2683